MASTERING

WORD PROCESSING

MACMILLAN MASTER SERIES

Banking
Basic Management
Biology
British Politics
Business Communication
Chemistry
COBOL Programming
Commerce
Computer Programming
Computers
Data Processing
Economics
Electronics
English Grammar
English Language
English Literature
French
French II
German

Hairdressing
Italian
Keyboarding
Marketing
Mathematics
Modern British History
Modern World History
Nutrition
Office Practice
Pascal Programming
Physics
Principles of Accounts
Social Welfare
Sociology
Spanish
Statistics
Study Skills
Typewriting Skills
Word Processing

MASTERING
WORD PROCESSING

P. E. GOSLING

MACMILLAN

First published 1985
Published by
Higher and Further Education Division
MACMILLAN PUBLISHERS LTD
Houndmills, Basingstoke, Hampshire
RG21 2XS and London
Companies and representatives
throughout the world

Typeset by
RDL Artset Ltd, Sutton, Surrey

Printed in Hong Kong

British Library Cataloguing in Publication Data
Gosling, P. E.
Mastering word processing.—(Macmillan
master series)
1. Word processing
I. Title
651.8   Z52.4
ISBN 0-333-36447-3
ISBN 0-333-36448-1 Pbk
ISBN 0-333-36449-X Pbk export

CONTENTS

PREFACE

When I put forward the suggestion that a worthy addition to the Master Series would be one on what word processing was all about I little knew how much hard work and research would be involved. It soon became obvious to me that the only way I was going to get to know each of the word-processing packages which I intended to describe was to write each section using that specific package. The Wordstar chapter was written first, since that is a word processor I use almost every day and that was easy. Then came the others and it soon became obvious that the task was formidable, very rewarding, but at the same time very time-consuming. Nevertheless it soon was soon clear that all word processors are much the same under the skin and reach similar goals by totally different routes. Five word-processing packages, I think, are enough to give the reader an idea of the kind of facilities offered and ways that word processors work.

The manuals supplied by computer companies offer different degrees of unreadability, do not always tell you the full story and rarely tell you how to get used to a particular word processor at what I call a 'trivial' level. This trivial level is one where you have to be able to type in a document, using the machine as you would a typewriter, and then perform simple editing on it. It is this feature which is covered in the first part of each chapter. Then the additional editing features are dealt with and the final part of each section is about how to control the way the document will look on the printed page and in particular how each word processor deals with the problem of producing personalised letters and address labels. Some allow you to do it very easily; some do it in a rather convoluted way. It is up to the reader to decide which particular method appeals.

In the production of this book I have been given a very large amount of help by friends and colleagues who have been most kind in allowing me to play with their word-processing packages in an attempt to get to grips with the problems each of them presents. In particular I must extend grateful thanks to my very good friends Roy Jones, Principal of Stamford College for Further Education, Steve Green of Midland Micro Services, John Davidson of QIS Computer Services, the directors of DTI Europe Ltd and Paul Smeeth, Managing Director of Elliott-Medway Ltd. All the photographs of screens have been taken by my son Patrick, but then taking photographs is now his bread and butter, so they ought to be good.

P. E. GOSLING

INTRODUCTION

1.1 WHAT THIS BOOK IS ABOUT

This book is an introduction to word processing and what various word processing systems are capable of. It is in no way intended to replace the comprehensive manuals which are supplied with each system. It is true to say that some of these manuals can be rather frightening for the new-comer and so this book provides, hopefully, a gentle lead-in to the full story which the manufacturers provide. This book attempts to provide an overview of some of the different ways by which a particular end result can be achieved and to show that although the paths to this result may differ considerably all word processors provide the same facilities in the long run. Ultimately all word processors are going to do the same thing. They all have to be able to delete sections of text, insert new text and move text about.

Some readers are going to say 'But why have you not included ...?' and might feel that their favourite word processor has been omitted. Someone is bound to feel left out since the number of word processors on the market is increasing daily and it is difficult to please everybody. This book is really aimed at the person who knows very little about word processing and wants to find out more in general terms. In fact, the idea of the book is not to highlight the differences between various systems but to bring out their similarities.

It is often felt, by people unfamiliar with this very useful application of the new technology, that there is so much to remember apart from the actual geography of the keyboard. In fact the keystrokes needed to perform the various word processing functions are usually easy to become familiar with as they generally fall into an easily remembered pattern. Many computer manufacturers are coming to realise that there is a great need for more 'user friendliness' and so more customised keyboards are being produced. These make life a great deal easier for the new user. Practice, as usual, makes perfect.

Once nice thing about word processors is that your typing speed and accuracy have no bearing on the quality of the final product. The computer is very tolerant of slow typists and will never tell you to hurry up while you are looking for a particularly elusive letter on the keyboard. All the author's books are now produced on a word processor and no one would flinch at the typing techniques used, except his wife who is a teacher of typing. The word processor will allow the mistakes which arise from two-finger typing to be amended with all speed and no one is the wiser.

Another facility which some word processors have is that of checking spelling. This is provided by a program which checks each word against entries in a 'dictionary' of several thousand words. If any word is found which is in doubt you will be informed and asked if the spelling is acceptable or not. If you agree that the word is misspelt then you can correct it. If on the other hand you say that is a valid word then it is added to the dictionary against its further use. This sounds a very time-consuming task. In fact it can take place very quickly indeed since it works on the 'roots' of words and the fact that a word with a 'root' such as 'love' can exist with many prefixes and endings so that love, loved, loving, unloved, lovable are all acceptable. However, 'luved' is not acceptable since 'luv' is not a 'root' word in the dictionary.

1.2 WHAT IS WORD PROCESSING?

In a letter to a woman's magazine recently a reader wrote that she was frightened of computers and that

> I was told by a computer addict that my plans for becoming an interpreter or translator were pointless. He said that word processors will soon replace the human . . . .

First of all I should like to reassure that lady and tell her that her fears are quite ungrounded. One can gauge the quality of the advice given by the adviser being described as a 'computer addict'. These so-called experts are among the worst advocates of the new technology and are prone to cloud the real issues with mythology and mumbo-jumbo. No wonder the average adult person is terrified of anything to do with computers. Of course, the popular press and television do not help a lot either. The advice the reader had been given was unfortunately typical of wrong thinking by the so-called computer enthusiasts who have a very narrow and highly coloured view of what computers can and cannot do. It is certainly unlikely in our lifetime, or even our children's, that computers will replace humans; at least in the sense that the writer of that rather pathetic letter fears.

There is no doubt that computers are already performing jobs which humans traditionally have done for many years. For example, quite small and cheap computers can handle all the invoicing and keep track of the financial transactions of a business; surely that can be no bad thing. Computers can help in financial planning – cash flow projections, for example – estimating and in many of the tasks which have bored generations of clerks to death over the past few hundred years. One particular job which I am personally very happy for a computer to take over is the production of the text for this book. I am not only a very poor typist both in speed and accuracy, but also I keep changing my mind about what I have written. In the past I presented my long-suffering publisher with a typed text which contained over-typing, written corrections and extra sheets clipped in the text numbered 39a, 40a, 40b, etc. Converting this into readable text must have been a very formidable task. I dare not give the text to my wife to type since not only can she not read my scribbled corrections and inserts to the text but she also flatly refuses to retype it all again when I find I need to change the text after it is supposed to be finished. Now that I use a word processor for all my writing I can type in my text as it comes to me, I always tend to type as I think, but I can amend, move around and add extra pieces of text knowing that I will obtain a perfect result every time.

Take the piece of text shown in Figure 1.1. It is presented exactly as I typed it in. There are spelling mistakes, pieces of text left out and other pieces needing to be inserted. A nightmare for a rotten typist such as myself. By the use of a word processor the text can be cleaned up and reprinted without having to retype it from start to finish, thus giving the result as shown in Figure 1.2.

Fig 1.1

One of the reasons for using compuktrers is to take that they can relieve us of away the boring (dull) and repetitive jobs and give them to a machine which is quite happy performing the type of task. This frees us to think about the things whiitch really maktter and offers us a way of improving the quality of life. provides us with the freedom

Fig 1.2

One of the reasons for using computers is that they can relieve us of dull, boring and repetitive jobs and allow us to give them to a machine which is quite happy performing this type of task. This provides us with the freedom to think about the things which really matter and offers us a way of improving the quality of life.

Another advantage of using a word processor when producing text for subsequent printing is that we can see exactly what it is going to look like on the printed page since word processors allow the lining up of the right-hand edge of the text – **justification** – by inserting the necessary spaces between the words so that each line is the same length. With a conventional typewriter we get a 'ragged' right-hand edge, but with a word processor we can clean it up and provide a very neat look to what is printed. For example, on a typewriter we would type the following:

```
Quite frankly, computers frighten me. Not only do they
threaten relationships, they threaten jobs. I was told
by a computer addict that my plans for becoming an
interpreter or translator were pointless: "Word
processors will soon replace the human, " he said.

The thought of wasting the years of studying another
modern language drives me to despair - was it really
all in vain?
```

But if typed on to a word processor the same text would be quite automatically set out like this:

```
Quite frankly,  computers frighten me. Not only do they
threaten relationships,  they threaten jobs. I was told
by  a  computer addict that my plans  for  becoming  an
interpreter   or   translator  were   pointless:   "Word
processors will soon replace the human, " he said.

The  thought of wasting the years of  studying  another
modern  language  drives me to despair - was it  really
all in vain?
```

A word processor can be used not only for editing text but also for storing and retrieving regularly used pieces of text. The editing of text makes use of the power of the computer to move data about inside its memory and the long-term storage of typed material is made possible by using the computer's **backing store** where it can permanently retain vast amounts of information. This is the more technical name given to the now familiar **floppy disks**. These are controlled by a device which is similar to a tape recorder, for recording music and speech. Vast amounts of information can be stored on magnetic disks, or sometimes magnetic tapes, recorded in just the same way as your domestic tape recorder stores the latest hit tunes or Beethoven's Fifth Symphony. To give some idea of the capacity of such disks, those attached to the computer being used to produce this text can each hold approximately 600 000 characters. That is equivalent to 165 pages of text of the size you are reading now. It therefore follows that if a secretary regularly has to produce standard letters for her boss she can store them on one of these magnetic disks and print them out whenever they are required. Having once typed a letter and stored it away, all that has to be done is to instruct the computer to select that letter from all the others on the disk and print it out. Additionally, there are many letters – lawyer's letters, quotations and contracts, for example – which are made up of a series of standard paragraphs. If these standard paragraphs, once typed, are stored away permanently on a disk then the typist has simply to tell the computer to assemble a complete letter from a selection of these standard paragraphs and then let it get on with the job.

Another task which can be left to a word processor is that of producing personalised letters from a mailing list. It is quite a simple task to write the letter once only, leaving gaps for the names and any other personalisation features. The computer will then merge in the names and addresses from a mailing list, kept on a disk of course, and print out as many letters as required. This accounts for the many 'free' gift offers which drop through your letter box appearing to be directed to you and you alone. In addition the same mailing list can be used to print the names and addresses on the envelopes, again quite automatically.

How this is done will be explained in the later sections of this book. You will find that it is in fact very easy. The drudgery of laboriously addressing hundreds of envelopes by hand is now a thing of the past.

1.3 USING A WORD PROCESSOR

So what do you need to be able to do in order to use a word processor? The answer is that so long as you know your way around a typewriter keyboard and are not afraid to experiment a bit then you are well on the way to processing your first word. You do not need to be a demon typist, you do not need to be a computer wizard and you must not, above all else, be scared of what might happen. It is most unlikely that you will hurt the computer in any way, destory all the files or make a fool of yourself. The best way to learn is to experiment and if you feel that is best done in secret away from the scorn of your more expert colleagues then do it that way. Nobody will mind. As with acquiring any skill, the more practice you have, the better at word processing you will become. At first you will feel that the number of things you have to remember and their complexity will be too much to grasp. Don't worry, you will soon gain confidence and speed as you gain experience.

The first thing you must learn is to use the keyboard properly. Basically, all computer keyboards are the same QWERTY type keyboards as a conventional typewriter. Figure 1.3 shows a standard typewriter keyboard and Figure 1.4 shows a typical computer keyboard. You should note that the real difference between the two is that the computer keyboard has a few more keys and there is often an additional numeric keypad on the right. There are three keys on a computer keyboard which have very

Fig 1.3 *standard typewriter keyboard*

Fig 1.4 *typical computer keyboard*

special significance. One of these is marked RETURN, sometimes RET or ENTER. This key performs the same function as the carriage return key on an electric typewriter or the carriage return lever on a manual typewriter. The other two keys are usually marked ESC, or ESCAPE, and CONTROL, CTRL or sometimes ALT. These keys have special functions which will be explained later. The 'touch' of a computer keyboard is fairly light and the keys respond equally well to a short 'dab' as to a firm press. Be warned, however, of pressing any key too hard. No, you won't hurt the keyboard, but you can cause the character shown on the screen, and hence transferred to the computer's memory to repeat. This only happens in certain keyboards. So make sure that you know what happens if you press a key and keep it down. A short, sharp tap on the key is normally all that is required.

Having investigated the keyboard the next part of your computer/word processor to examine is the screen. This is just like the screen of your television set except that it is used for the display of the text you are typing together with any information the computer needs to give you. It is the computer's way of communicating with you in the same way that the keyboard is your way of communicating with it. Linking the keyboard and the screen is the computer itself and this in its turn is connected to the magnetic disks which form the backing store. It is on this backing store that all the text you type in is filed away together with the program which 'drives' the word processor. A program is only a set of instructions, rather like a knitting pattern, but far less complicated!

The sequence of events which takes place when you use a word processor begins with starting the machine up so that it is told to remember the program of instructions. These tell it how to deal with everything you type in at the keyboard. This is done by loading the program instructions from the backing store into its memory. If the computer is designed to do this automatically as it is switched on and is incapable of executing any other sort ot program then it is known as a **dedicated word processor**. This means that it can only be used for this purpose and such a machine usually has a customised keyboard with keys marked 'Delete word', 'Delete line' and so on. The console of a dedicated system is shown in Figure 1.5 and a typical dedicated word processor is shown in Figure 1.6. This type of machine is usually only capable of performing the single task of word processing. Sometimes a dedicated system will be purpose-built and have a visual display unit so that a complete page of text can be seen at one time. Some even go so far as to turn the video tube on to its side so that the screen has the proportions of an A4 sheet of paper, and then the manufacturers make the display on the screen appear black on white in order to complete the illusion. This type of machine will, of course, be very expensive, around £10 000.

Fig 1.5 *console of a dedicated word processor*

A general purpose computer system is shown in Figure 1.7. The difference between the two is usually one of cost, the dedicated word processor usually costing more than a computer which runs a word-processing program. In a dedicated system you buy all the equipment as a package and this will usually consist of a desk, with the computer hidden away in it, and operator's console with screen and keyboard and a printer. A computer consisting of keyboard, screen and separate disk drives can be bought from a retailer who will suggest a suitable printer to match with it. Then you have a choice of program **packages** which will be run on that computer. One of these would be a word processing package, of which there were twenty-five listed for one well-known make of microcomputer

Fig 1.6 *a typical dedicated word processor*

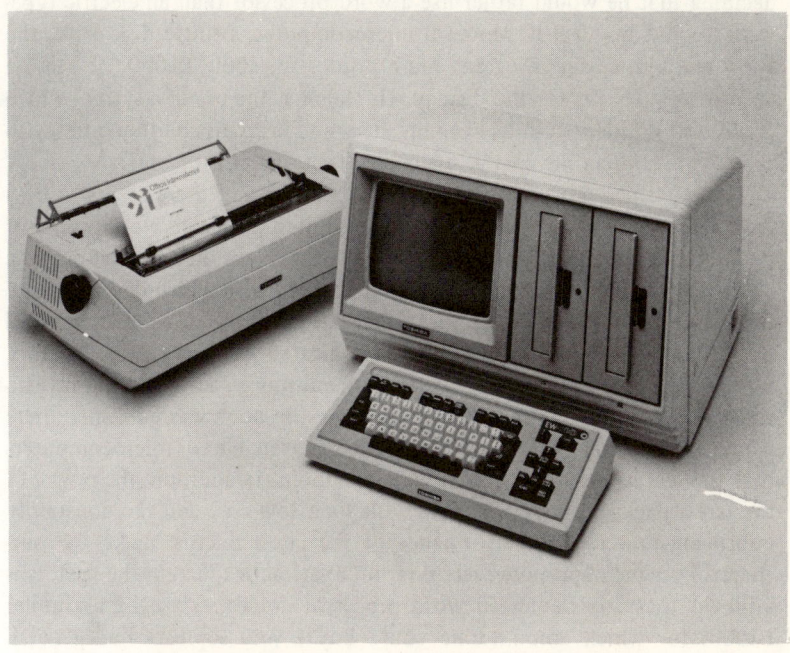

Fig 1.7 *a general purpose computer system*

alone in a recent magazine. Their cost, by the way, varied from under £100 to just over £400. As an example – for someone, say a writer, on deciding that he would rather use a word processor than an electric typewriter could buy a BBC Model B microcomputer, a single disk drive, the View word-processing program and a printer for about £1000. He can use an ordinary TV set for the display. He then has the use of a system which could also do his accounts, keep his diary and keep his children quiet with games for less than the cost of many electric typewriters.

It should perhaps be mentioned at this point that there seems to be a very definite swing away from the rather limited dedicated word processor towards the bought-in word-processing package used on a general-purpose microcomputer. To give some idea of the speed with which developments take place it should be noted that when this book was originally proposed it was intended to include a section on dedicated word-processing systems. But as the book started to grow in size and more packages were investigated it became very clear that by the time the book was published there would be so many word-processing packages available for microcomputers that the section would have become superfluous. In addition, the power of the latest packages in conjunction with their low cost and the constantly improving power/price performance of the latest micros, make the purchase of a general-purpose system far more attractive than in the past. It is unlikely that any dedicated word processor could be bought for under £4000, for which amount one could buy a very sophisticated general-purpose computer, a printer and a word processor such as Wordcraft or Applewriter together with other useful packages such as the spread sheet program, Visicalc.

In case the reader feels that a very strong case is being made against the dedicated type of machine it should be said that the potential user has to equate the trade-off of ease of use of one type against the low cost and flexibility of the other. The dedicated word processor will, of course, do its job superbly well and be very easy to get acquainted with. However, the price will usually put such a device out of the reach of the person at whom this book is aimed, namely the person who perhaps already has a mcirocomputer and is looking for an additional feature to add to it.

When using a computer for word processing we usually have to make do with pressing pairs of keys together or using certain keys for functions which have nothing to do with what is embossed on them. This is because the keyboard and the computer came first and then people wrote the word-processing programs to run on them. You will come across this occasionally confusing state of affairs with several of the systems described in this book, but in reality the systems are not really very difficult to get used to. With the new generation of small computers coming on to the market now it is possible to customise their keyboards, since the designers know that they are going to be used for word processing and so make sure they are easy to use. This means that many of the two-key functions are being programmed into special keys called **function keys** which are usually found along the top of the keyboard. A typical computer keyboard customised for use as a word processor is shown in Figure 1.8. This customising is particularly well done on the BBC microcomputer using VIEW, as the reader will see in the section devoted to that particular word-processing package.

Fig 1.8 *a typical 'customised' computer keyboard*

In case the reader fears that he or she has to become a computer expert in order to use a word processor, whether it be of the dedicated variety or a computer using a word-processing program, the answer is a very firm 'no'. After all, one does not need to know how a motor car works in order to drive to Birmingham on the M1 motorway. There is probably only one technical term which has to be understood when using a word processor and that is the term byte. This is just computer jargon for the amount of storage taken up by one single character; in other words, every time a key is struck on the keyboard one byte of information is transferred into the computer's memory. When you store a piece of text on a disk you are transferring the text which is held in memory on to the disk and each byte of information recorded on that disk represents one character of your text. Hence the 600 000 characters of text stored on a disk, as mentioned earlier, is referred to as 600K bytes. One K (for Kilo) is computer jargon for 'about one thousand' (actually 1024).

1.4 WORD PROCESSING IN ACTION

Finally, a résumé of the way in which we go about using a word processor and what we can use it for. Let us take one or two examples to illustrate the point. The first one takes place in a busy office.

The boss has returned from a meeting with a series of notes on various scraps of paper. She hands them to her secretary with instructions to type them up in the form of a report. The secretary reads through the notes and makes a few of her own, since the boss is not particularly good at spelling and her handwriting is not always very clear. She is aware, being a good secretary, of the boss's blind spots and can make an educated guess at what some of the scribbles mean. Having read through the original and made some sort of sense of it she goes over to her word processor, starts it up and inserts a disk into the disk drive as shown in Figure 1.9.

Fig 1.9 *inserting a disk into the disk drive*

This will probably be the disk which contains the word-processing program. She will also need to have a disk available on which the final report will be stored. Then she instructs the word processor to create a new document; this is the word processing equivalent of putting a new sheet of paper into the typewriter. She sets up, again just as she would on a typewriter, the width of the page, the positions of the margins and tabulator stops. Then she begins to type from her notes just as she would when using a type-writer, except that she does not have to worry about returning the carriage at the end of each line. Word processors have the ability to 'wrap' words round from the end of one line to the beginning of the next as soon as a line becomes full.

Having reached the end of the report our secretary can instruct the computer to display the document from the beginning, just as she typed it in. If she recognises any typing mistakes then they can be immediately corrected by deleting the incorrect characters and replacing them with the correct ones. Once she is satisfied with the first draft of the report it can be stored away on the disk. Then a printed copy of the report can be produced on the automatic printer attached to the word processor. This could be a daisy-wheel type of printer, as shown in Figure 1.10, or it could

Fig 1.10 *a daisy-wheel printer*

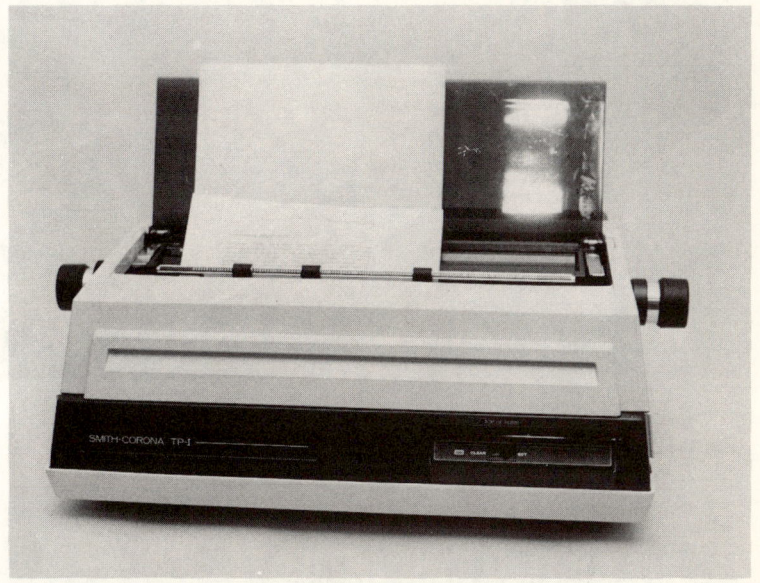

be a letter-quality dot matrix printer, as shown in Figure 1.11. The basic difference between the two methods of printing is that the former works in a similar way to a conventional typewriter in that each character is created by impact of a 'slug' of plastic on the end of a thin plastic arm, the characters being arranged rather like the petals of a daisy around a central spindle – see Figure 1.12. The latter works by a set of needles being 'fired' at the paper in various patterns in order to generate the characters. Having now obtained a printed copy of the notes the boss can write alterations and amendments on the paper. She may even want to change the order of certain paragraphs, and the secretary can recall the original text from the disk into the computer's memory and edit it, carrying out all the changes as required. There is no need for laborious retyping of the entire text; only the alterations need to be typed in. The word processor will re-form the text and make it look presentable again and the revised version can be stored in place of the orginal. Then a printed copy of the latest version of

Fig 1.11 *a letter-quality dot matrix printer*

Fig 1.12 *a daisy-wheel*

the text can be produced for approval and the process repeated until the boss is satisfied with the result.

The second example concerns sending a series of letters to a number of people on a mailing list. Usually a general letter has to be written. This letter is then duplicated on a photocopying machine with the salutation left in very general terms as, say, Dear Sir/Madam or Dear Subscriber, or a space is left for the name to be hand-written in. This method looks what it is, a compromise. Then comes the laborious task of addressing the envelopes. The next time a letter needs to be written to the same group of people the whole business has to be repeated. What most word processors allow us to do is to create a mailing list of names and addresses and then a single letter can be written with 'holes' in the appropriate places so that extracts from the mailing list can be inserted. For example, if we have a mailing list where we store all the information about out clients it would normally be on a card index filing system with information about the clients' names, addresses, telephone numbers and possibly some additional information about their jobs and status. We would normally have to manually extract the appropriate information required for any particular mail-shot from each of the cards. With a word processor this task becomes almost trivial.

How the various word processors in this book cope with this kind of operation is described in the appropriate sections. Each word processor deals with the task in a different way and with varying degrees of sophistication, but they all follow the same pattern, as you will see.

CHAPTER 2

WORDCRAFT

2.1 INTRODUCING WORDCRAFT 80

Wordcraft 80 (TM) is a word-processing package written to run on the
Commodore range of microcomputers and recently on the Sirius, Victor
and IBM PC machines. As with Wordstar (see Chapter 3) it requires a
computer with two disk drives. To start operations the master disk
containing the programs is placed in the right-hand disk drive, known to
Commodore as 'drive 0', and the door is closed. You should also ensure
that the **dongle** supplied with the program disc is plugged in. A dongle, by
the way, is a piece of solid state electronics which is essential for the run-
ning of Wordcraft, and is supplied to prevent illegal copying of the program taking place. If you press the keys marked SHIFT and RUN/STOP
simultaneously you will see the slightly cryptic message

```
dL "*"
loading
```

appear on the screen. This is quickly replaced by the Wordcraft 80 logo,
as shown in Figure 2.1. At this point you will need to enter a character
which informs the program of the printer type you are going to use. After
that has been done you will see the screen display as shown in Figure 2.2.
The four lines of this display tell you about the **status** of the text you are
preparing. The top line can display the date of creation of the text, the
name you have given it, the disk file name used for the document and
the number of the chapter you are working on. Wordcraft works in chapters, the maximum size of which is given by the number of 'chars free'
enumerated on the second line of the display. This tells you how many
characters you can store in memory at any one time for editing. When
the amount of free memory becomes small – it reduces with every keystroke you make – you will need to save the current document on disk
and commence work on the next chapter of the document. Apart from

Fig 2.1 *the Wordcraft 80 logo*

Fig 2.2 *initial screen display on Wordcraft 80*

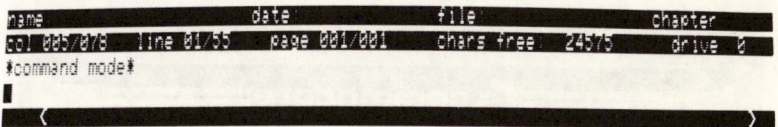

telling you how many characters you have left this line also tells you the exact position of the cursor in terms of the column number, the line number and the page number. For instance, 'col 033/078' tells you that you are at the 33rd column out of a possible 78, 'line 30/55' means that you are on the 30th line out of a possible 55 and 'page 001/005' means that you are on the first page out of five pages so far created. On the third line you are told which **mode** you are working in. At present you are in 'command' mode; the other two being 'type' mode and 'control' mode. The fourth line shows you the position of the margins of the 'page' you are working on together with any tab stops you may have inserted – but more of that later.

If you are in 'command' mode you are in a position to issue commands to the computer system in order to perform such tasks as printing out a document, saving it and retrieving it from disk. If you are in 'type' mode you are in a mode where everything you type becomes part of the document. Once you are in this mode you can type away just as if you are using an ordinary typewriter. The third mode is the 'control' mode which enables you to place control instructions into the document. The modes control the formatting of the final text; such things, for example, as the justification of the right-hand margin, indentation of paragraphs, tabbing and so on.

The **ruler line** at the top of the screen will have a '<' character at the left-hand end and a '>' character at the right-hand end; these are your margins and their positions can be altered at any time.

Before you actually start using Wordcraft 80 make sure that you can find the following keys as they are used extensively in this word-processor. They are:

RUN/STOP (Shifted for RUN, unshifted for STOP)
INST/DEL (Shifted for INST, unshifted for DEL)
OFF/RVS (Shifted for OFF, unshifted for RVS)
CLR/HOME (Shifted for CLR, unshifted for HOME)
ESC

making nine separate functions available in all. The keyboard is shown in Figure 2.3.

Fig 2.3 *Wordcraft 80 keyboard*

Before typing in your first document you can enter the current date by typing:

d=12/12/84

and you can name your document by typing:

n=mytext

when your screen will now look as shown in Figure 2.4.

Fig 2.4

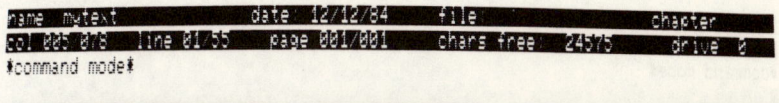

Next we have to get into 'type' mode and this is done by pressing the RUN/STOP key. You will see that *command mode* is immediately replaced by *type mode*. Then you can commence typing your text.

Start your exploration of Wordcraft by typing in the following:

```
In Wordcraft (TM) we have three 'modes' available to
us. These are called 'command' mode, 'type' mode and
'control' mode. The first of these allows us to do
things to the documents we create, such as calling them
into memory from disk, printing them, saving them away
on disk and naming them - very important - and so
on. The type mode is used when we actually use the
keyboard to enter text into a document. We can forget
that we are using a computer and just type away! There
is no need to return the carriage at the end of every
line, the word processor does that for us as soon as
it discovers that we have typed in more words than
there is room for on the line. Whenever we wish to
control the way our text will look on the printed page
we use the control mode. This enables us to create new
paragraphs, move text about, and insert blocks of extra
text into our document.
```

If by any chance you make a typing error all you need to do in order to delete the last character you have typed is to press the INST/DEL key. If you have found that you made a mistake in any part of the text already typed you can move the cursor around using the arrow keys which control its movement – they have CRSR on them and the appropriate arrows. To delete a character place the cursor over the unwanted character and press INST/DEL. Notice what happens to the rest of the text on that line when you do this. To insert an extra character in the text place the cursor at the place where you want the character to be inserted and press SHIFT and INST/DEL – that allows you to INSerT. Then type the character you wish to have inserted. Your screen should now look as shown in Figure 2.5. If you press the RUN/STOP key while in type mode, you are transferred back into command mode and at that point you might like to print the text you have just typed in. You do this by typing 'p'. Notice how the text is printed out with the right-hand margin justified. What you see on the screen is called **ragged text** but what is printed is called **justified text**. You can in fact control the justification feature by typing j=n (switches

20

Fig 2.5 *typed text on Wordcraft 80*

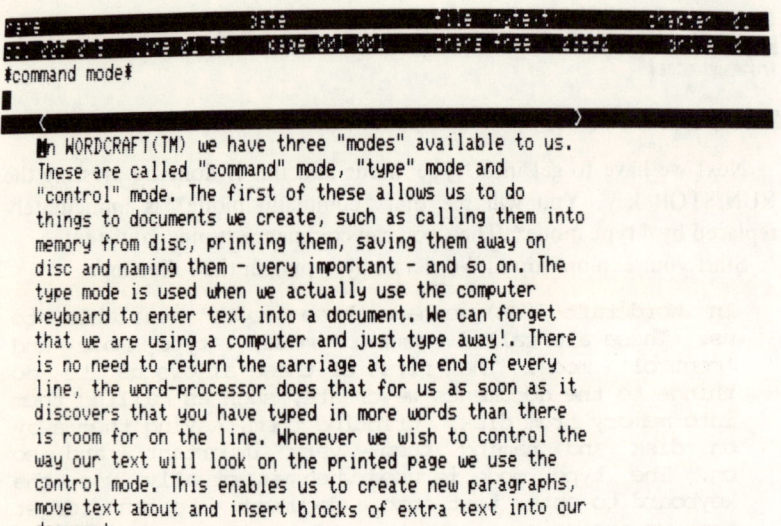

In WORDCRAFT(TM) we have three "modes" available to us.
These are called "command" mode, "type" mode and
"control" mode. The first of these allows us to do
things to documents we create, such as calling them into
memory from disc, printing them, saving them away on
disc and naming them - very important - and so on. The
type mode is used when we actually use the computer
keyboard to enter text into a document. We can forget
that we are using a computer and just type away!. There
is no need to return the carriage at the end of every
line, the word-processor does that for us as soon as it
discovers that you have typed in more words than there
is room for on the line. Whenever we wish to control the
way our text will look on the printed page we use the
control mode. This enables us to create new paragraphs,
move text about and insert blocks of extra text into our
document.

justification off) or j=y (switches justification on) while in command
mode.

If you want to insert more than one character into the text the easiest
way to do this is to place the cursor, using the arrow keys, at the beginning
of the inserted text and follow this by pressing RVS and INST. You will
see that a space opens up for you into which you can type your additional
text. At the end of the insertion press OFF (that is, SHIFT and RVS)
and the unused spaces are removed. To insert more text just press RVS
and INST again. Try this on the text you have already entered by adding:

> It does not matter how fast or how slowly we type, the word proces-
> sor will never try to hurry us along.

so that the text ends up looking like this:

> In Wordcraft (TM) we have three 'modes' available to us. These are
> called 'command' mode, 'type' mode and 'control' mode. The first
> of these allows us to do things to the documents we create, such as
> calling them into memory from disk, printing them, saving them
> away on disk and naming them – very important – and so on. The
> type mode is used when we actually use the computer keyboard to
> enter text into a document. We can foreget that we are using a
> computer and just type away! There is no need to return the carriage
> at the end of every line, the word processor does that for us as soon
> as it discovers that we have typed in more words than there is room

for on the line. It does not matter how fast or how slowly we type, the word processor will never try to hurry us along. Whenever we wish to control the way our text will look on the printed page we use the control mode. This enables us to create new paragraphs, move text about, and insert blocks of extra text into our document.

The sequence of events is shown in Figure 2.6, where we have opened up the space for the new text, Figure 2.7 where we have shown the text

Fig 2.6   *inserting new copy – space opened*

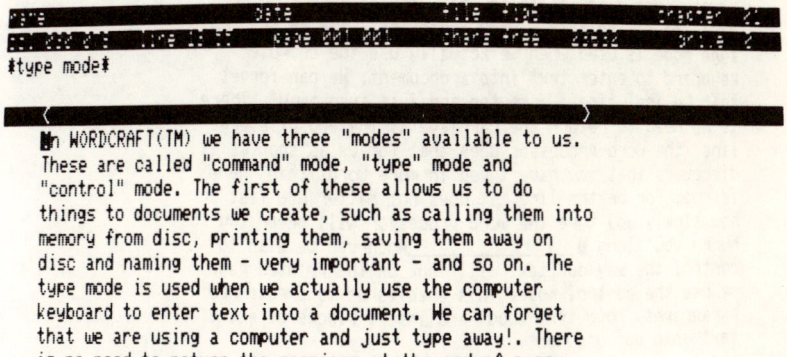

typed in – notice that you will have to open up two blanks in order to get all the extra text in. Figure 2.8 shows the new text with the gaps closed up.

If you wish to save your document away on disk you first have to get into command mode – press RUN/STOP for this – and type:

s,mytext,1,1

which will (s)ave the document under the name of 'mytext' on the disk in drive number 1 – first number – and it is the first chapter of the document. When the message

CHAPTER FILED OK

appears on the screen you know that you have successfully stored your document away. If you end your word-processing session by now typing

s,end

22

Fig 2.7 *inserting new copy – text typed in*

#type mode#

In WORDCRAFT(TM) we have three "modes" available to us.
These are called "command" mode, "type" mode and
"control" mode. The first of these allows us to do
things to documents we create, such as calling them into
memory from disc, printing them, saving them away on
disc and naming them – very important – and so on. The
type mode is used when we actually use the computer
keyboard to enter text into a document. We can forget
that we are using a computer and just type away!. There
is no need to return the carriage at the end of every
line, the word-processor does that for us as soon as it
discovers that you have typed in more words than there
is room for on the line. It does not matter how fast or
how slowly you type the word-processor will never try to
hurry you along.▮_____Whenever we wish to
control the way our text will look on the printed page
we use the control mode. This enables us to create new
paragraphs, move text about and insert blocks of extra
text into our document.

Fig 2.8

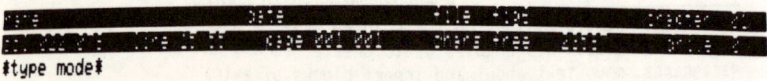

#type mode#

In WORDCRAFT(TM) we have three "modes" available to us.
These are called "command" mode, "type" mode and
"control" mode. The first of these allows us to do
things to documents we create, such as calling them into
memory from disc, printing them, saving them away on
disc and naming them – very important – and so on. The
type mode is used when we actually use the computer
keyboard to enter text into a document. We can forget
that we are using a computer and just type away!. There
is no need to return the carriage at the end of every
line, the word-processor does that for us as soon as it
discovers that you have typed in more words than there
is room for on the line. It does not matter how fast or
how slowly you type the word-processor will never try to
hurry you along. ▮henever we wish to control the way our
text will look on the printed page we use the control
mode. This enables us to create new paragraphs, move
text about and insert blocks of extra text into our
document.

you will have erased your document from memory, but luckily there is the copy still available on disk ready to be loaded. You can load it in again by typing

g,mytext,1,1   (the 'g' is for (g)et)

and the saved version of your text will be loaded from the disk into memory ready for further editing. If you have loaded a document from disk into memory and changed it in any way – you may have amended sections or even added extra text on to the end – you save it again by typing:

s,mytext,1,1,r

where the 'r' at the end informs the computer system that it has to (r)eplace the previous version of 'mytext' with a revised one.

The author, always one for never asking others to do what he would never dream of doing himself, has written this section using Wordcraft on a Commodore 8032 microcomputer. It has proved just about the right length for a 'chapter' since at the start there were 10005 characters free and now there are 1295 free, so it is about time this section was filed away by typing:

s,wordcraft,1,1

and clearing out the memory by typing:

n   (for (n)ew)

and starting off on section 2.2.

2.2 USING WORDCRAFT CONTROL COMMANDS

The control commands offered by Wordcraft provide a wide range of very easy to use yet sophisticated operations. The easiest to use and understand is the command to produce a new paragraph. Because Word-craft carries on wrapping text round from line to line as we proceed through our document we have to tell it to halt from time to time in order to allow us to commence a new paragraph. After typing the final character at the end of the line which finishes one paragraph we press the OFF/RVS key and this takes us into control mode. Then we press RETURN and the cursor is positioned at the start of the next line. We do not need to 'un-control' since the action of pressing the RETURN key automatically takes us back into type mode. Now, most paragraphs do not simply follow on one after the other; there is usually a blank line separating successive paragraphs. So press OFF/RVS and RETURN again and you will see that there is now a blank line after the last sentence of the previous paragraph so that the layout of our document is easily controlled. Most other word processors allow us to press RETURN on its own for a new line – sometimes it is even called a 'NEW LINE' key – but Wordcraft insists that we do it from control mode. What is actually happening is that codes are placed into the text, which does not have great gaps left in it in the interest of economical use of space on disk and in memory, and these are recognised by the part of the word processor which controls the printing and its layout. Hence the need to say 'the next character is a printing control character'.

An easy control code to start practising with is the one which controls the width of the text. To set the left-hand margin we enter control mode by pressing OFF/RVS and then the # character. The word RULR appears at the top of the screen, as shown in Figure 2.9. Then the cursor is moved

Fig 2.9 *setting margins – RULR prompt*

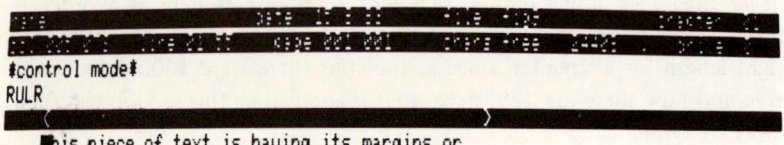

to the position where we require the left-hand margin to be and the < key is pressed. Now move the cursor to the position where the right-hand margin is to be. This time press the > key. Press RVS again to get back to type mode. Figure 2.10 shows a revised left-hand margin in the 10th column and the right-hand margin at the 50th column.

Fig 2.10 *revised margins*

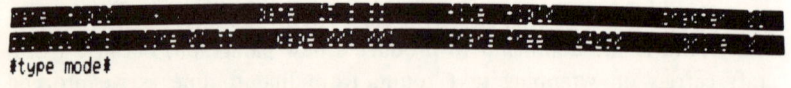

Text typed in with the left margin at column 7 and the right margin at column 64 will look like this.

Tab stops are set in the same way as the margins except that we use the '↑' character to specify the tab positions. Up to sixteen tab stops are allowed in a ruler line. To delete a tab stop we press RVS # again and line the cursor up at the stop we wish to delete. Then '←', the left arrow at the top left of the keyboard, will delete that tab stop. If we press RVS # followed by \, the **backslash** character, all the tab stops are deleted. Don't forget that RVS again takes you back into type mode. To start text at a tab position press RVS t or RVS TAB and the cursor jumps to the next tab position.

Decimal tabs can be used to set up tables of numbers with all the decimal points arranged under one another as shown below:

```
  23.45              456.789
 456.78                  .001
1234               1235.036
```

In order to do this we press RVS . (the full stop character) instead of RVS TAB. A screen layout using tab stops is shown in Figure 2.11.

Fig 2.11 *a screen layout using tab stops*

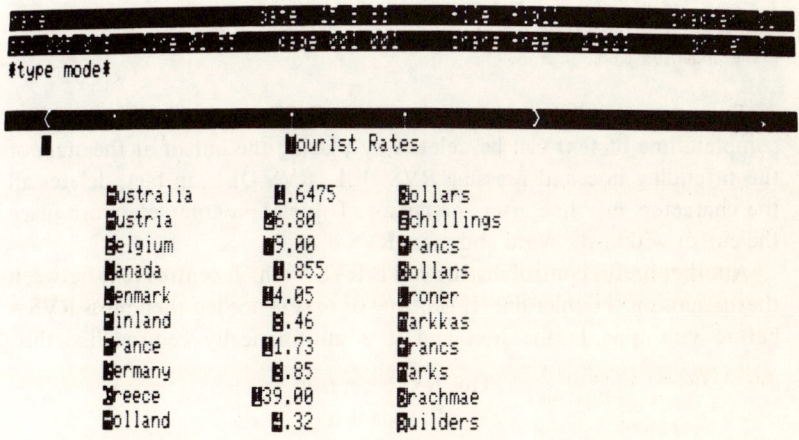

Another feature for which we can use the ruler line is that of indentation. This allows a section of text to be indented within the overall margins.

For example, this text is written using indentation controls forcing the left-hand margin to be at the position of the extreme left-hand tab stop. This is done by pressing RVS [before typing the indented text and saves having to hit RVS TAB at the start of each line of the text to be indented. Indentation is switched off by typing RVS] after you have gone on to a new line after the indented text.

The effect on the ruler line of the RVS [control is shown in Figure 2.12. RVS [saves us having to amend the margins temporarily.

Fig 2.12 *the effect of the R VS [control*

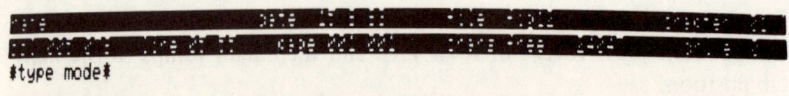

In this example we are going to indent a section of
text within the overall margins. We use RVS [for
this:-

        Now I can start typing in another paragraph
        indented to the position indicated by the
        previously set up tab position, but this is
        converted into a new margin by the [character,
        which I have to press before I type in the
        indented text.

I have now switched off the indentation by going onto
a new line and pressing RVS]. This saves me having
to press RVS TAB at the start of every new line on
the indented text.

To insert a section of text we use RVS INST, as mentioned already. A complete line of text can be deleted by placing the cursor at the start of the offending line and pressing RVS DEL. RVS DEL, in fact, deletes all the characters in a line after the cursor. To delete a complete word place the cursor within the word and press RVS d.

Another useful control instruction is RVS = which centres text between the margins on the ruler line. If centring of text is needed then press RVS = before you type in the text and it is automatically centred like this:

This text is centred
and so is this

Unlike Wordstar (see Chapter 3) the Wordcraft command *precedes* the centred text.

One of the important features of any word processor is that which will allows us to look for specific strings of characters in a document. The control command to do this is RVS s. You are then asked for the string you are searching for. You type this in and enclose it in '' marks as shown in Figure 2.13. The cursor will then move, and very quickly too, to the

Fig 2.13   *the command to search*

```
#control mode#
SRCH "search█
```
```
 his is a piece of text in which we show how the
command to search looks. We use it in this example
to find the word "search" in this text. note that
the cursor has to be positioned in front of the
character string being searched for, otherwise to
search will fail.
```

selected string as soon as you have typed the second '' character. If the string cannot be found then you will see a message to the effect. Having found a string you may wish to replace it by another string. For example in the following text

In our country we drive on the left of the road.

We want to change the word 'left' for 'right', so we press RVS s and the word SRCH appears on the screen. We reply with "left" and as soon as the right-hand '' has been keyed in the cursor is on the first character of the word searched for. If we now press RVS x the word EXCH appears. Now if you key in "right" the exchange is made. If we pressed RVS z instead of RVS x we would exchange the words every time the searched word is found. If we write the text

In the theatre there are three main areas. These are the stage, the auditorium and the backstage area. To me the backstage area is by far the most interesting. Here all is usually bustle and rush despite the apparent calm of the actors on the stage. It is up to the backstage staff to ensure, whatever panic they may be in, that the audience sitting in the auditorium is amused and entertained.

and then wish to change every occurrence of the word 'the' into the word 'a' we would get this:

In a aatre are are three main areas. Ase Are a stage, a auditorium and a backstage area. To me a backstage area is by far a most interesting. Here all is usually bustle and rush despite a apparent calm of a actors on a stage. It is up to a backstage staff to ensure, whatever panic ay may be in, that a audience sitting in a auditorium is amused and entertained.

Not quite what was intended! That is because the word searched for and replaced was embedded inside words which were not intended to be altered. What should have happened is that the searched word should be specified as "the   " with a space at the end so that we would then get:

> In a theatre there are three main areas. These are a stage, a auditorium and a backstage area. To me a backstage area is by far a most interesting. Here all all is usually bustle and rush despite a apparent calm of a actors on a stage. It is up to a backstage staff to ensure, whatever panic they may be in, that a audience sitting in a auditorium is amused and entertained.

But note that there are still things which we had not really bargained for resulting from that amendment of the text, so beware!

To move about a page of text we use the arrow keys, but these do not allow us to move about across page boundaries. To do this we use RVS p, which produces a PAGE prompt. If we now press either the up or down arrow we can flick either back to the previous page or forward to the next page. To go directly to a specific page we press RVS P followed by the page number required. However, for some reason known only to the authors of Wordcraft, any page number greater than 9 has to be enclosed in brackets.

If we press RVS followed by one of the arrow keys we can 'pan', or scroll automatically, through the text. The prompts PANU, PAND, PANL and PANR (up, down, left and right) appear in the command line and the text scrolls quite quickly in the appropriate direction. The panning can be stopped by pressing RVS again. The left and right pan operations are useful if very wide documents are being prepared, that is, ones which are more than eighty characters wide and so cannot have complete lines on the screen.

RVS p HOME takes us to the start of the chapter and RVS p CLR takes us to the last character in the document.

Control codes are used for moving text about and reproducing the same piece of text in various parts of the same document. In fact, this technique was used in the production of the previous example. There was no point in laboriously typing out the same text three times. We mark a block of text by placing the cursor at its start and pressing RVS m if we wish to move the text bodily, RVS r if we want to reproduce the text elsewhere and RVS e if we want to erase the block of text. As we do this a 'block identify' message comes on to the screen. Then we move the cursor to the position after the last character in the block and press RVS and SHIFT (i.e. OFF). This causes a block position message to display. Now the block has been marked at its beginning and its end. Then we place the cursor at the position where we want to reproduce the text and press OFF again. In a matter of seconds the text appears in its new position.

Finally, to save this section I type:

s,mytext,1,2

signifying that it is the second chapter of the file called 'mytext' to be saved on drive 1.

2.3 PRINTING INSTRUCTIONS

We issue commands to Wordcraft in order to tell it how we wish to have our document printed out. In section 2.1 we saw that by the command 'p' we can cause the current 'chapter' to appear on the printer, but there is more to it than that. For example, we may wish to put 'headers' and 'trailers' on to the printed page. These are the short pieces of text at the top and bottom of every page that you see in many books. To place a header text at the start of every page we press 'h' while in command mode and the prompt *header* appears on the third line from the top of the screen. We can then type in the text we require to have printed at the top of every page. After pressing RETURN this instruction is kept ready for the time when the printing takes place. In the same way we can press 't' and the prompt *trailer* appears. Then, as the page number is usually placed in this position and this is inserted by RVS p, at which point three 'p' characters, highlighted, appear. If there needs to be some text as well, this can be typed in. In the case of this section of the book the trailer text was the word 'Page' and the page number. There are variations on this theme, but these can be gleaned from the main manual and experimented with. It is a nice feature that the first chapter has pages numbered from 1 to the end and the second and subsequent chapters, without any prompting from us, carry on the page numbers properly in sequence.

To print the chapter currently in memory we press 'p', but if we only want to print certain pages from that chapter we press p,1-3 if, for example we wish to print pages 1, 2 and 3.

If we press p,3 we will print all the pages from page 3 onwards. If we press p,-3 we will print all pages up to and including page 3.

Now it is quite common that we should want to print certain parts of our text either underlined or in bold type. Wordcraft gives us the opportunity to provide one or other, but not both, of these facilities. Underlined text is prefixed by RVS <. It is terminated by RVS > or any paragraph break or page break character. This produces what Wordcraft called 'highlighted' text. When printed out such text will be underscored. However, if at the time of printing the type:

p,1-2,b

the underscored characters are printed in bold type instead.

If we want to set out the text in double spacing, as one would with a draft document which needs checking before a final print takes place, we can specify that double spacing is required by the command:

p,required pages,d

If several copies of a document are required then this can be specified at printing time by adding a number at the end of the printing instructions. It might also be noted at this point that there has to be a page number definition after the 'p' and before the 'b' or 'd'. So that if we issue the print instruction:

p,,b,2

we mean that we want two copies of every page, with emboldened text. If we type:

p,,d,3

we require three copies of everything in double spacing. The command:

p,2-5,,2

means that we want two copies of pages 2 to 5 of the current chapter with no special printing instructions.

The next thing to get Wordcraft to do for us is to send out personalised letters and mailing lists for which the names and addresses are taken from a file stored on disk quite separately from the 'skeleton' letter. We store the data in the form shown in Figure 2.14. This means that we create a separate file with each field of the record relating to a person, or whatever, set on a new line. This is done by typing each field followed by RVS & with the final field terminated by the 'new page' command which is RVS HOME. Each field is then separated by a line of dashes:

- -

Each field is referenced by a letter. The first field in each record is known as A, the second as B and so on. The skeleton letter is laid out with blanks referencing the field to be placed into it at any point. The insertion point is marked by RVS ? followed by the field reference letter. The skeleton used for our example is shown on the next page.

The results from the command:

f,waddres,1,1-3 (the 1-3 tells Wordcraft to fill with records 1 to 3)

are shown in Figure 2.15. There is one letter for each person on the file. The address file, called 'waddress' in this case, has already been written and then saved. The 'f' command means that the document currently

```
* * *
                              U.T.C.Trading Co.,Ltd.,
                              U.T.C.House,
                              Wharton.
                              Norfolk.
                              NR4 6QT


5th May 1984

 ~A ~B ~C
 ~D.
 ~E.
 ~F


Dear ~A ~C

We  are pleased to.  inform you that we now have a new  range  of
computer  accessories in stock and have pleasure in enclosing our
latest  catalogue.  As  a valued customer of ours over  the  past
years.  ~A ~C, we will be pleased to offer you and  extra  5%
discount on all orders placed with us during the current month.


Yours very sincerely.


J.Barton
Sales Manager
```

```
* * *
```

in memory, namely the skeleton letter file, is to be 'filled' from the 'fill' file, namely 'waddress'. The same 'fill' file can be used to provide, for example, address labels and a telephone number list by using the skeleton documents shown below:

```
~A ~B ~C.
~D.
~E.
~F
```

Similarly, a telephone list would be:

```
~A ~B ~C : Telephone number: ~G
```

and that short document would produce selected fields from the same file in yet another form. There are many opportunities for using a word processor with this kind of facility. Some suggestions are found in the appendix at the end of this book. For example, by typing RVS ? RVS a space can be created where extra text, or a name, can be inserted at the time the document is printed. The letter shown below was prepared like this.

* * *

Dear ˇ.

I am pleased to hear that ˇ is now recovered from ˇ illness. Please pass on my best wishes to ˇ.

Yours as always,

* * *

Fig 2.14 *data for mailing list*

```
Dr.
----------------------------------------------------------------
F.G.W.
----------------------------------------------------------------
Hardy
----------------------------------------------------------------
Westfield Road
----------------------------------------------------------------
Salisbury
----------------------------------------------------------------
Wiltshire
----------------------------------------------------------------
0567-32456



Mr
----------------------------------------------------------------
P.K.L.
----------------------------------------------------------------
Thomas
----------------------------------------------------------------
Lincoln Road
----------------------------------------------------------------
PETERBOROUGH
----------------------------------------------------------------
Cambs
----------------------------------------------------------------
0733-4766



Lord
--------------------------------------------------------------
Peter
--------------------------------------------------------------
Wimsey
--------------------------------------------------------------
Railway Cuttings
--------------------------------------------------------------
East Cheam
--------------------------------------------------------------
Surrey
--------------------------------------------------------------
01-789-9999
```

Fig 2.15 *the completed letters*

* * *

```
                        U.T.C.Trading Co.,Ltd.,
                        U.T.C.House,
                        Wharton,
                        Norfolk,
                        NR4 6QT
```

5th May 1984

Dr. F.G.W. Hardy
Westfield Road,
Salisbury,
Wiltshire

Dear Dr. Hardy

We are pleased to inform you that we now have a new range of computer
accessories in stock and have pleasure in enclosing our latest catalogue.
As a valued customer of ours over the past years, Dr. Hardy, we will be
pleased to offer you an extra 5% discount on all orders placed with us
during the current month.

Yours very sincerely,

J.Barton
Sales Manager

* * *

* * *

```
                        U.T.C.Trading Co.,Ltd.,
                        U.T.C.House,
                        Wharton,
                        Norfolk,
                        NR4 6QT
```

5th May 1984

Lord Peter Wimsey
Railway Cuttings,
East Cheam,
Surrey

Dear Lord Wimsey

We are pleased to inform you that we now have a new range of computer
accessories in stock and have pleasure in enclosing our latest catalogue.
As a valued customer of ours over the past years, Lord Wimsey, we will be
pleased to offer you an extra 5% discount on all orders placed with us
during the current month.

Yours very sincerely,

J.Barton
Sales Manager

* * *
```
```

34

Fig 2.15 continued

* * *

```
                    U.T.C.Trading Co.,Ltd.,
                    U.T.C.House,
                    Wharton,
                    Norfolk,
                    NR4 6QT
```

5th May 1984

```
Mr P.K.L. Thomas
Lincoln Road,
PETERBOROUGH,
Cambs
```

Dear Mr Thomas

We are pleased to inform you that we now have a new range of computer
accessories in stock and have pleasure in enclosing our latest catalogue.
As a valued customer of ours over the past years, Mr Thomas, we will be
pleased to offer you an extra 5% discount on all orders placed with us
during the current month.

Yours very sincerely,

```
J.Barton
Sales Manager
```

* * *

This letter is shown on the screen in Figure 2.16. To print a personalised
version of the letter, go into type mode and press RVS f. This opens up a
space after the first 'tick' and you can enter your own words. You might

Fig 2.16

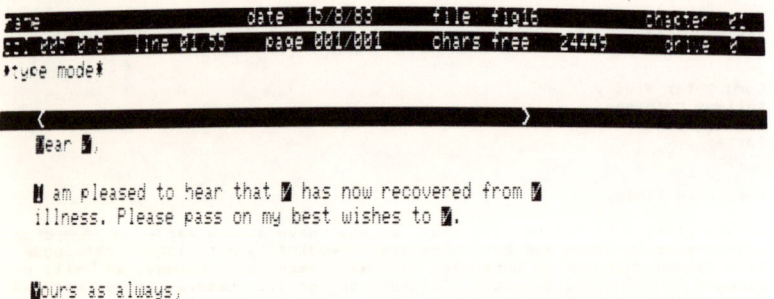

notice that the tick which appears on the screen gets printed out as another
character, in this case the tilde character, on the printer. Press RVS f again
and the next space opens up and so you can fill up the blanks in the letter.
When you have finished this press SHIFT OFF and print the whole letter.

You will get something like this:

* * *

Dear Mary,

I am pleased to hear that Uncle George is now recovered
from his illness. Please pass on my best wishes to him
and Aunt Jane.

Yours as always,

* * *

Wordcraft 80 is a powerful word-processing package but has the disadvantage of using rather complicated control codes which are somewhat bewildering to the newcomer. The embedded control codes take quite a lot of getting used to and as there are no 'help' menus available the user always has to return to the manual to find out what has caused things to go wrong. Searching and replacing facilities are fast and very easy to use, and the production of personalised letters from mailing lists is very easy also. The text is not formatted on the screen and so the user cannot preview exactly how the document is going to look in its final form. One advantage, though, is that the document currently in memory can be printed immediately without having to be saved away on disk first.

CHAPTER 3

WORDSTAR

3.1 **INTRODUCING WORDSTAR (TM)**

Wordstar (TM) is a very powerful and sophisticated word-processing package – a *package* is computer jargon for a program or set of programs which will run, generally, on a range of computers. This particular package is available for all microcomputers which can run the CP/M operating system and have at least 48K of RAM. CP/M (Control Program for Microcomputers) is a registered trade mark of Digital Research Inc. Wordstar exists in various versions and the latest version, the one used in this book, is known as Version 3.00. Like all good packages it is **user friendly** and the user is guided by a series of **menus**. One of the comforting things about Wordstar is that one can use it at a simple level within seconds of it being loaded into memory.

The usual sequence of events needed to use Wordstar is first to load the Wordstar disk into the main drive of your computer and then carry out the start-up procedure. This is bound to differ from computer to computer and will depend on how the manufacturer has organised the 'booting-up' of the system. What usually happens is that after the boot-up procedure a prompt in the form of a letter A and the > character appear on the left-hand side of the screen:

     A>

At that point the computer is awaiting a command and this is usually indicated by the bright rectangle known as the **cursor** sitting immediately after the > character – sometimes the cursor will blink on and off to attract your attention. In order to obtain Wordstar you will usually have to respond by typing the letters 'WS' followed by the RETURN, CAR. RET or ENTER key. When you press this key it is your way of transferring control to the computer system. The first thing to happen after the main part of Wordstar has been loaded into memory is that the 'commercial' will appear briefly on the screen telling which version of the package you have and its serial number. After a few seconds this will fade and be replaced by the 'no-file menu'. The only keys which will cause Wordstar to do anything are those listed in the menu. If you press any key other than L, F, H, D, N, P, E, O, Y, R, X, M or S nothing will happen. Try pressing, say, the key A and see what happens, then press the key F and see the result. If you press the key L you can transfer to another disk drive, say drive B. The screen display you might get is shown in Figure 3.1. Notice that beneath the menu is what is called the **directory** or disk B. This is list of the contents of the disk, known in computing circles as the **file-names**. Everything stored on a disk is known as a **file**. If you have a completely fresh, new Wordstar disk the directory of drive A will only contain the files known as WS. CMD (sometimes WS. COM), WSMSGS. OVR, MAILMRG. OVR (if you have bought the MAIL-MERGE option) and WSOVLY1. OVR. Make sure that these are present. If they are not, your system is not likely to work. Notice that there is hardly ever any need to press the RETURN key when using Wordstar.

Press F again and observe the result. The menu shown in Figure 3.1 is one you will always return to when a piece of text editing has been completed. It is your way into and out of Wordstar. It is usual with most word processors to have the programs which drive the word-processing program on the master drive and the documents which you create on the other drive.

Fig 3.1 *Wordstar screen display*

```
          editing no file
                <<< N O - F I L E   M E N U >>>
   ---Preliminary  Commands---   | --File  Commands-- | -System  Commands-
 L  Changed logged disk drive    |                    |  R  Run a Program
 F  File directory   off (ON)    |  P  Print a file   |  X  EXIT to system
 H  Set help level               |                    |
  ---Commands to open a file---  |  E  RENAME a file  | -WordStar Options-
    D  Open a  document  file    |  O  COPY   a file  |  M  Run MailMerge
    N  Open a non-document file  |  Y  DELETE a file  |  S  Run SpellStar

DIRECTORY of disk A:
 DEMO.ASM    DEMO.PRN     DEMO1.ASM    DEMO1.PRN    DEMO1.BAK     FIG310
 FIG311      FIG312       FIG317       FIG320       FIG331        FIG332
 FIG333      FIG335       FIG338       FIG339       FIG340        FIG342
 FIG344      FIG38        FILEMARK.CMD FTPPAT.ASM   FTPSANYO.ASM  LETTER
 LETTER1     LINK.SUB     LOG.ASM      MINE         MYTEXT.BAK    TW.BAS
 LIST.INT    DEMO.HEX     DEMO1.HEX    A.COM        ASM.COM       COMPARE.COM
 DDT.COM     DEMO.COM     DEMO1.COM    DT.COM       DUMP.COM      ED.COM
 FORMAT.COM  FTP.COM      GENHEX.COM   LASTERR.COM  LIST.COM      LOAD.COM
 MAPIT.COM   MMFORMAT.COM MMSYSGEN.COM RECLAIM.COM  RXA.COM       S.COM
 TXA.COM     VERIFY.COM   WS.COM       MAILMRGE.OVR WSMSGS.OVR    WSOVLY1.OVR
```

The first thing you need to do is to become familiar with the way a **document** is prepared – a document is the name given to a piece of text, whether it be a letter, report, contract or a complete book. Press the D key and you will be asked for the name given to the document. This is shown in Figure 3.2. Respond with the name you wish to call your document, with not more than eight characters in the name (no spaces) as the

Fig **3.2** *naming the document*

instructions in Figure 3.2 tell you. Suppose we call our document by the name 'MYTEXT'. As you are going to create a new document Wordstar will recognise this and produce the screen display as shown in Figure 3.3. The symbols across the screen just below the menu represent the left and right margins and the ! characters represent tab stops. These are all set up for you by Wordstar and can be modified very simply. You will notice that across the top of the screen is a line of text which tells you that you are using a disk in drive A – that is the 'A:' in front of your chosen document name – and information telling you where the cursor is currently positioned. The page normally contains 66 lines and each line is normally 65 characters long. These can be altered very simply by you.

At this point do not worry about the menu displayed, just type in the following text. Do not worry about returning the carriage as you would with a typewriter at the end of lines. Wordstar takes care of all that for you by placing the text on a new line as soon as the current line is filled. Just keep typing. Wordstar will set up a clean right-hand margin for you by inserting extra blanks in the text in order to achieve justification:

This is a test piece of text to show you how easy it is to use the Wordstar package. You can type as fast or as slowly as you like, speed it not essential. If you do make a mistake don't worry. You will soon be shown how to edit mistakes out of a piece of text.

The use of a word-processing package enables you to produce error-free text with the minimum of effort and without lengthy retyping of the text every time a change has to be made.

Fig 3.3 *menu for document creation*

The new paragraph, by the way, is started by pressing the RETURN key. This makes the cursor go to the beginning of the next line. You can indent the first word of the new paragraph by pressing the space bar until the cursor is where you want it. There are other ways, but we will deal with them later. Notice that when you have pressed the RETURN key a < symbol appears on the right-hand side of the screen to remind you that you have included what is called a 'hard' carriage return.

Your screen should now look as shown in Figure 3.4. Even if you have made some errors do not worry about them at this point. We will come to the way to correct errors and insert extra text later on.

What has to be done now is to arrange for the text to be stored away on a disk for subsequent printing or further editing. If you now press what we

Fig 3.4 *test piece of text displayed*

call 'control K' we will be able to issue one of a series of instructions which are indicated on the menu shown in Figure 3.5. Control K is achieved by pressing the key marked CONTROL, CTRL or sometimes ALT together with one of the keys specified in the menu. The only ones we shall concern ourselves with at this point are the keys S, D, X and Q. Note that pressing control K is indicated by the characters '^K' being displayed in

Fig 3.5 *saving the text*

the top left-hand corner of the menu. The ^ symbol in front of a letter indicates that the control key is depressed at the same time as the letter key. Release the CONTROL key and press S. What will happen is that the text will be saved on disk and the cursor repositioned at the start of the text. Notice that the screen prompt you get after the saving has taken place tells you to press ^QP to reposition the cursor at its last position. This means that you can continue with the editing of your text. The reason for this is that it is a good idea to save your text at regular intervals just in case something happens which would cause you to lose the results of many hours of work.

Now type the additional text shown on to the end of your document so that you end up with the following:

This is a test piece of text to show you how easy it is to use the Wordstar package. You can type as fast or as slowly as you like, speed it not essential. If you do make a mistake don't worry. You will soon be shown how to edit mistakes out of a piece of text.

The use of a word-processing package enables you to produce error-free text with the minimum of effort and without lengthy retyping of the text every time a change has to be made. Control keys enable us to instruct Wordstar to perform certain operations on the text. Control K supplies us with a set of instructions which can, among other things, allow text to be stored on disk.

When you have typed in the extra text press ^K again but follow it this time by D. Now you will see that your text has not only been saved but this time you have been taken out of the editing mode and returned to the 'No-file' menu. If you look at the list of saved files under the menu you will see that your text exists in not one but two files. One is called 'MYTEXT' and the other called 'MYTEXT.BAK'. The second of these is what is called a 'back-up' copy and is in fact the original text you typed in. This means that your text is stored on the disk in two versions; one is the currently saved version and the back-up is the previously saved version. This means that if you have made so many errors in the latest version that it has to be abandoned then you can return to the previous version and start your editing afresh. In order to see that this is the case, press D and call up the text file called 'MYTEXT. BAK'. You should get the instruction shown in Figure 3.6 which tells you that before editing a .BAK file you have to rename it – E command – or copy it into another file to be named by you – O command. The effect is the same in both cases. If you rename it you simply change the file name from 'MYTEXT. BAK' to, say, 'NEWTEXT'. If you copy you take a copy of 'MYTEXT. BAK' and call

Fig 3.6 *rename or copy instruction*

```
         editing no file
            < < < N O - F I L E   M E N U > > >
      ---Preliminary Commands---  : --File Commands--  : -System Commands-
   L  Changed logged disk drive   :                    :  R  Run a Program
   F  File directory   off (ON)   :  P  Print a file    :  X  EXIT to system
   H  Set help level              :                    :
      ---Commands to open a file---:  E  RENAME a file   : -WordStar Options-
   D  Open a  document file        :  O  COPY   a file   :  M  Run MailMerge
   N  Open a non-document file     :  Y  DELETE a file   :  S  Run SpellStar ▌

   Can't edit a file of type .BAK or .$$$
   -- rEname or cOPY before editing


   Partial DIRECTORY of disk A:  ^Z=scroll up
   DEMO.ASM     DEMO.PRN     DEMO1.ASM    DEMO1.PRN    DEMO1.BAK    FIG310
   FIG311       FIG312       FIG317       FIG320       FIG331       FIG332
   FIG333       FIG335       FIG338       FIG339       FIG340       FIG342
   FIG344       FIG38        FILEMARK.CMD FTPPAT.ASM   FTPSANYO.ASM LETTER
   LETTER1      LINK.SUB     LOG.ASM      MYTEXT       MYTEXT.BAK   TW.BAS
   LIST.INT     DEMO.HEX     DEMO1.HEX    A.COM        ASM.COM      COMPARE.COM
   DOT.COM      DEMO.COM     DEMO1.COM    DT.COM       DUMP.COM     ED.COM
   FORMAT.COM   FTP.COM      GENHEX.COM   LASTERR.COM  LIST.COM     LOAD.COM
```

the copy, say, 'NEWTEXT'. In the second case you will retain the original back-up copy and can start editing 'NEWTEXT'. Try both copying and renaming now. The screen prompt tells you everything you need to do and will tell you if you have made an error. If you have got yourself into a position where you want to abandon editing a document you get out of the editing mode with ^K followed by Q for 'quit'. In this case there is no saving of the current document and you will get the screen prompt shown in Figure 3.7.

There is one more useful thing we can do from the 'no-file' menu and it concerns the printing of a document. If you refer to Figure 3.1 you will see that printing is controlled by the P key – press P to print a document. If you do this you will see that you are asked for the name of the file you wish to print. Type this in and you will see that you are asked the question

DISK FILE OUTPUT (Y/N):

and you press the ESC key at this point. There are many other things you can do here, but while you are getting to know Wordstar it is probably better to use the simplest available commands.

3.2 EDITING A DOCUMENT

By now you should be able to create a document, save it on disk and print it on printer attached to the computer. Now we come to editing an existing text and the commands needed to move the cursor about the text so that

Fig 3.7 *screen prompt for abandoning a file*

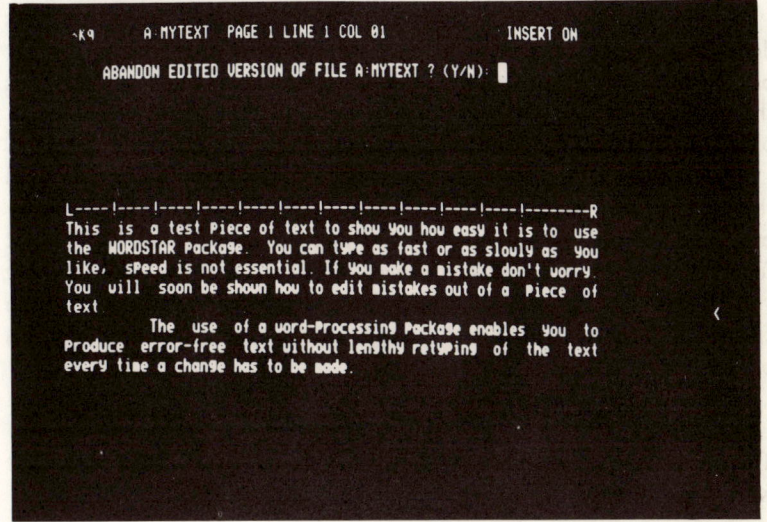

we can insert new text, delete unwanted text and move text about within the document. If you refer to the menu shown in Figure 3.3 you will see a list of commands which control movement of the cursor. At first sight you might think that their choice is haphazard and that it is going to be a difficult task to remember what their functions are. In fact, it is very easy because the four key control functions are handled by the keys E, X, S and D which are arranged on the keyboard as follows:

```
        ---
       !E!
      -----
    !S! !D!
      -----
       !X!
        ---
```

By pressing ˆE (control E) the cursor moves up one line, ˆX moves the cursor down one line, ˆD moves it one character to the right and ˆS moves it one character to the left. Notice that the movement of the cursor is related to the relative positions of the four keys and so their functions are quite easy to remember. This 'star' of keys is the key to Wordstar. Call up a document and practise moving the cursor about the text. When you have gained confidence you can extend your cursor movement by using the keys to the left of the S and the right of the D. ˆA moves the cursor one **word** to the left and ˆF moves it one **word** to the right. Notice that you cannot move the cursor outside the defined limits of the text. In other

44

words you cannot move the cursor to a place before the first character in the text or after the last character in the text.

Another feature Wordstar gives us is that of **scrolling** the text. This is done by using the keys W, R, Z and C. Notice how they fit into the star pattern as well. ^W moves the text on the screen down one line, ^Z moves the text up one line, ^C moves about three-quarters of the screen up at once and ^R moves the same amount down.

Notice that at the top of the "main menu" in Figure 3.3 you are told the name of the file you are working on, the position of the cursor by page, line and column and whether the 'insert' function is on. If the insert function is on it means that wherever the cursor is in the text anything you type will be inserted at that point and the text to the right of the cursor will be pushed further to the right as you type in new text. Try this out by typing in:

This shows us how to insert new text into existing text

Then move the cursor back to the first 't' in the first occurrence of the word 'text'. Then type:

portions of

so that you will get:

This shows us how to insert new portions of text into existing text as is shown in Figure 3.8. The line now has more characters in it than our line length permits so we have to re-form it.

Fig 3.8 *inserting new portions of text into existing text*

We re-form the text by placing the cursor at the start of the text – over any character in the first word ('This' in this case) – and give the command ^B and the text is re-formed and the cursor is positioned over the last character in the text. Thus we get the text displayed as in Figure 3.9.

Fig 3.9 *re-forming the text*

```
        A:FIG38  PAGE 1 LINE 2 COL 06              INSERT ON
                   < < <     M A I N   M E N U     > > >
        --Cursor Movement--     : -Delete- :   -Miscellaneous-  :  -Other Menus-
    ^S char left ^D char right :^G char  : ^I Tab   ^B Reform : (from Main only)
    ^A word left ^F word right :DEL chr l!: ^V INSERT ON/OFF  :^J Help  ^K Block
    ^E line up  ^X line down   :^T word rt!^L Find/Replce again:^Q Quick ^P Print
        --Scrolling--          :^Y line   :RETURN End Paragraph:^O Onscreen
    ^Z line up   ^W line down  :          : ^N Insert a RETURN :
    ^C screen up ^R screen down:          : ^U Stop a command  :
    L----!----!----!----!----!----!----!----!----!----!----!--------R
    This  shows  us how to insert new portions of text into  existing
    text.█
```

Now we are in position to insert new text, what about deleting parts of the text, single characters, complete words or complete lines?

If you call up a document to the screen and place the cursor somewhere in the middle of it you will see that ^G will delete the character under the cursor, ^T will delete the word, or part of a word, to the right of the cursor and ^Y will delete the complete line. If you press the DEL key you delete the character to the left of the cursor.

To switch the Insert function off you need the ^V command. If you do this you will see that you are in effect 'over-typing'. The effect is shown in Figures 3.10 and 3.11. ^V again switches 'Insert' on again.

There is, of course, more to editing and amending text than just typing in new sections or deleting them. For example, it is very common for us to need to re-form a letter of an article by changing the order of paragraphs. This can easily be done, as can a number of other very useful operations, by using the ^K commands. These commands are all associated with 'blocks' of text. In fact, if you press ^K and watch the menu display on the screen, as in Figure 3.12 you will see what is available. This is the block menu. We have already seen how ^KD allows us to save a document on disk. We will now see what the effects of ^KD, ^KK, ^KC and ^KV are.

Fig 3.10 *deleting text*

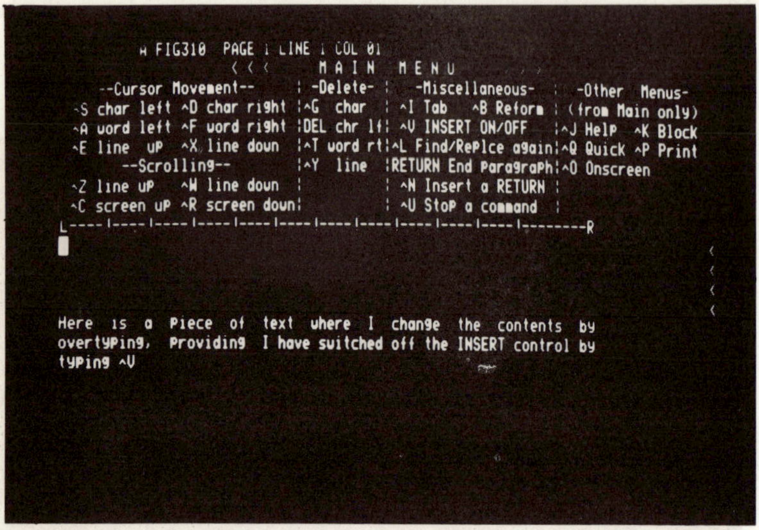

Fig 3.11 *deleting text*

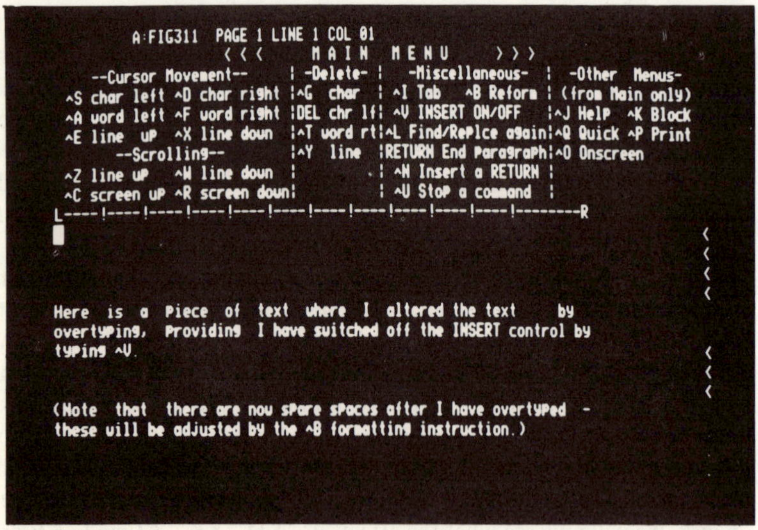

Fig 3.12 *block menu*

```
^K     A:FIG312  PAGE 1 LINE 1 COL 01          INSERT ON
                 < < <      B L O C K   M E N U      > > >
 -Saving Files- : -Block Operations- : -File Operations- :   -Other Menus-
S Save & resume : B Begin  K End      : R Read  P Print   : (from Main only)
D Save--done    : H Hide / Display    : O Copy  E Rename  : ^J Help  ^K Block
X Save & exit   : C Copy   Y Delete:  J Delete            : ^Q Quick ^P Print
Q Abandon file  : V Move   W Write    : -Disk Operations- : ^O Onscreen
 -Place Markers-: N Column on (OFF):L Change logged disk: Space Bar returns
0-9 set/hide 0-9:                    :F Directory on (OFF): you to Main Menu.
L----!----!----!----!----!----!----!----!----!----!----!--------R




 ▉his is a test piece of text to show you how easy it is to  use
the WORDSTAR package. You can type as fast or as slowly as  you
like, speed is not essential. If you make a mistake don't worry.
You will  soon be shown how to edit mistakes out of a  piece  of
text.                                                             <
         The use  of a word-processing package enables you  to
produce  error-free  text without lengthy retyping of  the  text
every time a change has to be made.
```

First of all call up the document we have already created called 'MYTEXT'.
Place the cursor at the start of the first paragraph in front of the word
'This'. Press ^KB, and you will see the display shown in Figure 3.13. Then
place the cursor after the last character of that paragraph. Then press ^KK.

Fig 3.13 *first step in moving a block of text*

```
       A:FIG312  PAGE 1 LINE 1 COL 01          INSERT ON
                 < < <      M A I N   M E N U      > > >
    --Cursor Movement--    : -Delete- :   -Miscellaneous-  : -Other Menus-
 ^S char left ^D char right :^G char  : ^I Tab   ^B Reform : (from Main only)
 ^A word left ^F word right :DEL chr lf: ^U INSERT ON/OFF  :^J Help  ^K Block
 ^E line up  ^X line down   :^T word rt:^L Find/Replce again:^Q Quick ^P Print
    --Scrolling--           :^Y line  :RETURN End Paragraph:^O Onscreen
 ^Z line up  ^W line down   :         : ^N Insert a RETURN :
 ^C screen up ^R screen down:         : ^U Stop a command  :
L----!----!----!----!----!----!----!----!----!----!----!--------R




 <B>▉his is  a test piece of text to show you how easy it is to  use
the WORDSTAR package. You can type as fast or as slowly as  you
like, speed is not essential. If you make a mistake don't worry.
You will  soon be shown how to edit mistakes out of a  piece  of
text.                                                             <
         The use  of a word-processing package enables you  to
produce  error-free  text without lengthy retyping of  the  text
every time a change has to be made.
```

The screen will look like that shown in Figure 3.14. Some versions of Wordstar will produce highlighting. This depends on the characteristics of the video monitor you are using. Next place the cursor on the first line after the end of the second paragraph and press ^KV. The text will

Fig 3.14 *second step in moving a block of text*

```
       A:FIG312  PAGE 1 LINE 5 COL 06              INSERT ON
                  < < <     M A I N   M E N U     > > >
      --Cursor Movement--    ! -Delete- !  -Miscellaneous-  ! -Other  Menus--
 ^S char left ^D char right !^G char  ! ^I Tab   ^B Reform ! (from Main only)
 ^A word left ^F word right !DEL chr l! ^V INSERT ON/OFF   !^J Help ^K Block
 ^E line up  ^X line down  !^T word rt!^L Find/Replce again!^Q Quick ^P Print
       --Scrolling--       !^Y  line  !RETURN End Paragraph!^O Onscreen
 ^Z line up   ^W line down !          ! ^N Insert a RETURN !
 ^C screen up ^R screen down!         ! ^U Stop a command  !
L----!----!----!----!----!----!----!----!----!----!----!--------R



 <B>This  is  a test piece of text to show you how easy it is to  use
 the  WORDSTAR Package.  You can type as fast or as slowly as  you
 like,  speed is not essential. If you make a mistake don't worry.
 You  will  soon be shown how to edit mistakes out of a  piece  of
 text.<K>█                                                          <
       The  use  of a word-processing package enables  you  to
 produce  error-free  text without lengthy retyping  of  the  text
 every time a change has to be made.
```

now appear as it is in Figure 3.15. This command has allowed us to move text from one part of our document to another. The pair of commands ^KB and ^KK mark the beginning and end of a block of text within our document. Having marked the block we can move it or we can copy it from one part of the document to another by using ^KC – 'Copy'. The difference between copying and moving should be clear once you have tried it once or twice.

The ^KR command allows us to call in documents and insert them into our current document and so we are able to construct letters from standard paragraphs which have previously been stored on disk. For example, try the following exercise:

1. Create and save the following document under the name PARA1:
   You have exceeded your credit limit and we regret that we can no longer supply you with further goods.

2. Create and save the following document under the name PARA2:
   We are pleased to inform you that you have credit available on your account and the goods you have ordered will be dispatched as quickly as possible.

Fig 3.15 *moving a block of text completed*

```
        A:FIG312  PAGE 1 LINE 6 COL 01              INSERT ON
                 < < <     M A I N   M E N U    > > >
     --Cursor Movement--    : -Delete- :  -Miscellaneous-  : -Other Menus-
   ^S char left ^D char right :^G char  : ^I Tab  ^B Reform : (from Main only)
   ^A word left ^F word right :DEL chr l: ^V INSERT ON/OFF  :^J Help  ^K Block
   ^E line  up  ^X line down  :^T word rt:^L Find/Replce again:^Q Quick ^P Print
     --Scrolling--           :^Y line  :RETURN End Paragraph:^O Onscreen
   ^Z line up   ^W line down  :         : ^N Insert a RETURN :
   ^C screen up ^R screen down:         : ^U Stop a command  :
   L----!----!----!----!----!----!----!----!----!----!----!--------R


            The  use  of a word-processing package enables you  to
     produce  error-free  text without lengthy retyping  of  the text
     every time a change has to be made.

     <B>This  is  a test piece of text to show you how easy it is to use
     the  WORDSTAR package. You can type as fast or as slowly as  you
     like,  speed is not essential. If you make a mistake don't worry.
     You  will  soon be shown how to edit mistakes out of a  piece  of
     text.<K>
```

3. Create the following document and save it under the name LETTER:

Union Trading Co.,
New Street,
Newtown,
Middlesex.

ADDRESS
ADDRESS
ADDRESS
ADDRESS

DATE

Dear

Thank you for your order for further supplies.

Yours faithfully,

J. P. Smith,
Managing Director

What you are now going to do is to create a letter which contains the current date, the appropriate name and address and an inserted paragraph according to your wishes as you have two alternative paragraphs to insert. As you are going to modify an existing outline letter you will first need to cOpy it into a new document command (O). This allows you to retain the original for further use. Copy LETTER into a document called LETTER1. Now load LETTER1 and when you have done so switch 'Insert' off (^V command). It should look as shown in Figure 3.16. Because you have

Fig **3.16** *loading LETTER1*

```
                  A LETTER1  PAGE 1 LINE 7 COL 01
        L----!----!----!----!----!----!----!----!----!----!--------R
                                        Union Trading Co.,        <
                                        New Street,               <
                                        Newtown,                  <
                                        Middlesex                 <
                                                                  <
        ■DDRESS                                                   <
        ADDRESS                                                   <
        ADDRESS                                                   <
      ' ADDRESS                                                   <
                                                                  <
        DATE                                                      <
                                                                  <
        Dear                                                      <
                                                                  <
        Thank you for you order for further supplies.             <
                                                                  <
        Yours faithfully,                                         <
                                                                  <
        J.P.Smith                                                 <
```

switched off the insertion mode you can overtype the name and address of the recipient of the letter in the places indicated. Then you will have a screen which looks like that shown in Figure 3.17. You can easily type the salutation after the word 'Dear' and then place the cursor after the first line of the letter and type ^KR. You will then be asked for the name of the file to read – you can type either PARA1 or PARA2 depending on the type of letter you wish to send – see Figures 3.18 and 3.19. Before you print the letter you have now created you will have to save it – ^KD first and then P for the printing to commence. If you want to retain the complete letter on disk you may do so. If not once you have printed the letter you may delete it – command. There are other ways of providing this personalised form of letter but the method shown here is the simplest to use, and enables you to practise using Wordstar commands.

Now we come to another way in which we can alter text. This is by using ^QA which enables us to find certain sets of characters and replace

Fig 3.17 *letter with address overtyping*

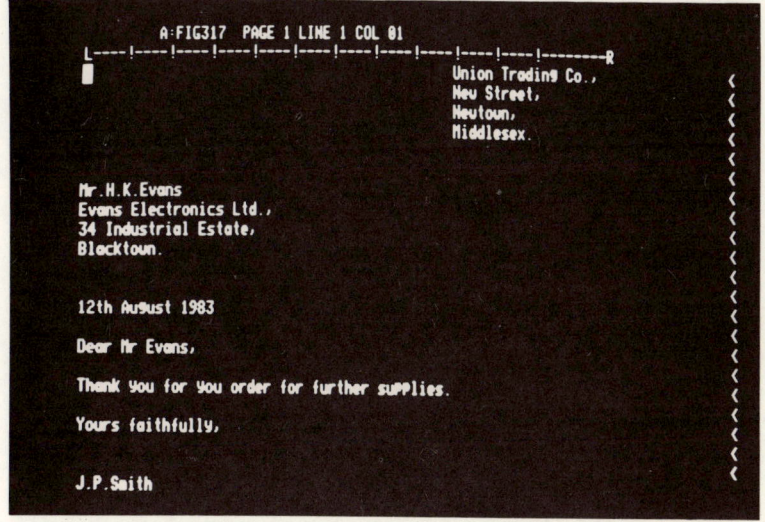

```
        A:FIG317 PAGE 1 LINE 1 COL 01
    L----!----!----!----!----!----!----!----!----!----!--------R
    ▯                              Union Trading Co.,      <
                                   New Street,            <
                                   Newtown,               <
                                   Middlesex.             <
                                                          <
    Mr.H.K.Evans                                          <
    Evans Electronics Ltd.,                               <
    34 Industrial Estate,                                 <
    Blacktown.                                            <
                                                          <
    12th August 1983                                      <
                                                          <
    Dear Mr Evans,                                        <
                                                          <
    Thank you for you order for further supplies.         <
                                                          <
    Yours faithfully,                                     <
                                                          <
    J.P.Smith                                             <
```

Fig 3.18 *letter version 1*

```
                                    Union Trading Co.,
                                    New Street,
                                    Newtown,
                                    Middlesex.

    Mr.H.K.Evans,
    Evans Electronics Ltd.,
    34 Industrial Estate,
    Blacktown


    12 August 1984

    Dear Mr Evans,

    Thank you for your order for further supplies.

    We  are  pleased  to  inform you that  you  have  credit
    available  on  your  account and  the  goods  you  have
    ordered will be despatched as quickly as possible.

    Yours faithfully,

    J.P.Smith,
    Managing Director
```

Fig 3.19 *letter version 2*

```
                              *  *  *

                              Union Trading Co.,
                              New Street,
                              Newtown,
                              Middlesex.

Mr.H.K.Evans,
Evans Electronics Ltd.,
34 Industrial Estate,
Blacktown


12 August 1984

Dear Mr Evans,

Thank you for your order for further supplies.

You  have  exceeded your credit limit and we regret that
we can no longer supply you with further goods.

Yours faithfully,


J.P.Smith,
Managing Director

                              *  *  *
```

them with others. Call up the document you have already created called
MYTEXT. Then type ^QA and you will have a screen which looks as
shown in Figure 3.20 where it asks you what set of characters you wish to
find and subsequently replace. Choose a word, or even a single character,
you wish to replace and when you have typed it in press RETURN. You
are then asked what the replacement is to be. Having entered the replacement characters and pressed RETURN again you will be given a series of
options – obtained only if you press '?'. The choice of a backwards or
forwards search is useful if you have the cursor at the 'wrong end' of a
document. You can specify how many times you can make Wordstar
find and replace and you can arrange for the operation to take place with
or without intervention by you. The options can be combined by responding with, say, 10B if you want the searching to take place backwards
from the present cursor position and to repeat the operation 10 times
only. If you type WNG you will replace whole words only (W), without
being asked (N) and in the entire file (G). The ability to replace whole
words only is so that if you wanted to replace every occurrence of the
word 'the', for example, you would want to avoid doing this in words such
as 'theatre' or 'breathe'. You should practise with this facility on text you
have created to get used to using it.

Fig 3.20   *replacing characters*

```
^Qa      A:FIG320  PAGE 1 LINE 1 COL 01

^S=delete character   ^Y=delete entry   ^F=File directory
^D=restore character  ^R=Restore entry  ^U=cancel command

   FIND? █




L----!----!----!----!----!----!----!----!----!----!----!--------R
This is a test piece of text to show you how easy it is to use
the WORDSTAR package.  You can type as fast or as slowly as you
like,  speed is not essential. If you make a mistake don't worry.
You will soon be shown how to edit mistakes out of a piece of
text.
        The use of a word-processing package enables you to
produce error-free text without lengthy retyping of the text
every time a change has to be made.
```

3.3 OTHER MENUS

Wordstar commands are arranged under a series of menus, of which we have already seen two. These are the "main", no "No-file", menu shown in Figure 3.1 and the 'K' or Block, menu which is displayed whenever 'control K' is pressed; this was shown in Figure 3.5. Each of these menus covers a specific range of Wordstar functions. Probably the most useful to the novice is the 'J' menu. This is a menu which contains helpful information about how Wordstar is used. If you press 'control J' you will find that the menu at the top of the screen changes to that shown in Figure 3.21. Pressing any one of the keys H, B, F, D, S, R, M, P or V will give information about a range of functions.

For example, if once having pressed 'control J' you follow it with R you will get information about how the ruler line at the top of the screen is used to lay out the text. This is shown in Figure 3.22. If you press the space bar you are returned to the main menu and you can carry on with your text entry.

You see from the J, or help, menu that ^OL controls the position of the left-hand margin and likewise ^OR controls the position of the right-hand margin, so that you can alter the width of your 'page' and the positions of the margins by these commands. In addition, the tab stops can be cleared with ^ON and set with ^OI. This is easy to try out. First of all

Fig 3.21 *help menu displayed*

```
^J       A:FIG320  PAGE 1 LINE 8 COL 36
              < < <     H E L P   M E N U     > > >
                                    :            : --Other  Menus--
   H  Display & set the help level  : S  Status line   : (from Main only)
   B  Paragraph reform (CONTROL-B)  : R  Ruler line     :
   F  Flags in right-most column    : M  Margins & Tabs : ^J  Help  ^K  Block
   D  Dot commands, Print controls  : P  Place markers  : ^Q  Quick ^P  Print
                                    : V  Moving text    : ^O  Onscreen
                                    :                   : Space Bar returns
                                    :                   : You to Main Menu.
   L----!----!----!----!----!----!----!----!----!----!----!--------R
   This is a test piece of text to show you how easy it is to use
   the WORDSTAR package. You can type as fast or as slowly as you
   like,  speed is not essential. If you make a mistake don't worry.
   You will soon be shown how to edit mistakes out of a piece of
   text.
           The use of a word-processing package enables you  to
   produce  error-free  text  without lengthy retyping of the text
   every time a change has to be made.█
```

Fig 3.22 *ruler line information*

```
          M FIG320  PAGE 1 LINE 8 COL 36
              ***** RULER LINE *****

   L----!----!----!----!----!----!----!----!--------R

   L    Left margin (set with ^OL)
   R    Right margin (set with ^OR)
   !    regular tab stop (set with ^OI, clear with ^ON)
   #    decimal tab stop (set with ^OI, clear with ^ON)
   -    other positions between margins

                   Press space bar after reading: █
   L----!----!----!----!----!----!----!----!----!----!--------R
   You  will  soon be shown how to edit mistakes out of a piece of
   text
           The use of a word-processing package enables you to
   produce  error-free  text  without lengthy retyping of the text
   every time a change has to be made.
```

press 'control O' and N and you get the instructions as shown in Figure 3.23. It asks you which tabs you wish to clear. If you press A you clear them all. Try that and you get a screen which looks like that shown in Figure 3.24. Note that the ! symbols which represent tab stops have all

Fig 3.23 *clearing tabs*

Fig 3.24 *tabs cleared*

vanished. Now press 'control O' and R and it asks you for the column in
which you want to have the right-hand margin. Reply with, say, 55 and
you will see that the width of the page has been reduced so that its extreme
right-hand edge is at column 55. 'Control O' and L will allow you to

change the position of the left-hand margin to whatever you wish. Change it to 10 and you should get a ruler line as shown in Figure 3.25. You can now put tab stops in at whatever positions you like by 'Control O' and I.

Fig 3.25 *new margins set*

You are asked where you want to place a tab stop; reply with, for example, 20. If you press the ESCAPE key you will have a tab stop placed wherever the cursor happens to be at that time. If you place a tab stop in column 20 you will find that the cursor will move immediately to column 20 so that all paragraph indentations, for example, will be at the same place without tedious counting on your part. Your screen will now look as shown in Figure 3.26.

You can, of course, place as many tab stops along a ruler line as you wish and treat them in exactly the same way as you would treat tab stops on a typewriter. If you want to enter columns of figures and ensure that all the decimal points are lined up correctly you can use decimal tab stops. Press 'Control O' and I and then before telling Wordstar where you want to place the tab stop press the # key; it might be the English pound sign on some keyboards. Then you can enter the column number. Place a decimal tab in column 35 and you should have a ruler line as shown in Figure 3.27. Now enter some text at the tab stop in column 20 and numbers at column 35. Just press the tab key, enter the text and then press it again and enter a number. Press RETURN and do the same on the next line. You will find that the numbers you enter are automatically lined up in the correct

Fig 3.26 *new tabs set*

```
                    A MYTEXT  PAGE 1 LINE 1 COL 01
                        < < <    M A I N   M E N U    > > >
        --Cursor Movement--  : -Delete- :  --Miscellaneous-  :  -Other Menus-
     ^S char left ^D char right :^G char  : ^I Tab   ^B Reform : (from Main only)
     ^A word left ^F word right :DEL chr lf: ^V INSERT ON/OFF  :^J Help  ^K Block
     ^E line  uP  ^X line down  :^T word rt:^L Find/RePlce again:^Q Quick ^P Print
          --Scrolling--        :^Y line   :RETURN End Paragraph:^O Onscreen
     ^Z line uP   ^W line down  :          : ^N Insert a RETURN :
     ^C screen uP ^R screen down:          : ^U StoP a command  :
            L---------!----------------------------------R
```

This is a test Piece of text to show you how easy it is to use
the WORDSTAR PackaGe. You can tyPe as fast or as slowly as you
like, sPeed is not essential. If you make a mistake don't worry
you will soon be shown how to edit mistakes out of a Piece of
text.
         The use of a word-ProcessinG PackaGe enables you to
Produce error-free text without lengthy retyPing of the text
every time a chanGe has to be made.

Fig 3.27 *placing a decimal tab*

```
                    A:FIG327  PAGE 1 LINE 1 COL 01
                        < < <    M A I N   M E N U    > > >
        --Cursor Movement--  : -Delete- :  --Miscellaneous-  :  -Other Menus-
     ^S char left ^D char right :^G char  : ^I Tab   ^B Reform : (from Main only)
     ^A word left ^F word right :DEL chr lf: ^V INSERT ON/OFF  :^J Help  ^K Block
     ^E line  uP  ^X line down  :^T word rt:^L Find/RePlce again:^Q Quick ^P Print
          --Scrolling--        :^Y line   :RETURN End Paragraph:^O Onscreen
     ^Z line uP   ^W line down  :          : ^N Insert a RETURN :
     ^C screen uP ^R screen down:          : ^U StoP a command  :
            L---------!--------------8-------------------R
```

columns as shown in Figure 3.28. This is obviously of great use when producing price lists and estimates.

The 'J' menu is, as you will have seen, used to give you help while you are using Wordstar so that you do not have to be constantly referring to

Fig 3.28 *column of figures with decimal tab*

the manual. However, when you have become fairly adept at using the program you will feel that this constant prompting and hand-holding is rather superfluous. You can switch off the helping hand of the 'J' menu whenever you like and in fact you can switch it off a bit at a time by setting various 'help levels'. There are four of these with help level 3 being the most detailed and help level 0 allowing none of the help menus to be displayed at all. To change help levels you type 'control J' followed by H. You will then be able to select the level of help you require, as shown in Figure 3.29. When you start Wordstar you are automatically at help level 3. Going down to help level 2 means that the main menu is no longer permanently present at the top of your text; all you get is as is shown in Figure 3.30, but the separate menus obtained from 'control J', 'control K', etc., still appear. To suppress these menus you need to go down to help level 1, so that when you press 'control K', 'Control P' and so forth you get no reminder of what the characters which follow these codes will do. By going down to level 0 all explanations are suppressed. You can easily go from level to level and see which suits you best as you become more and more fluent in using Wordstar.

Fig 3.29 *selecting help levels*

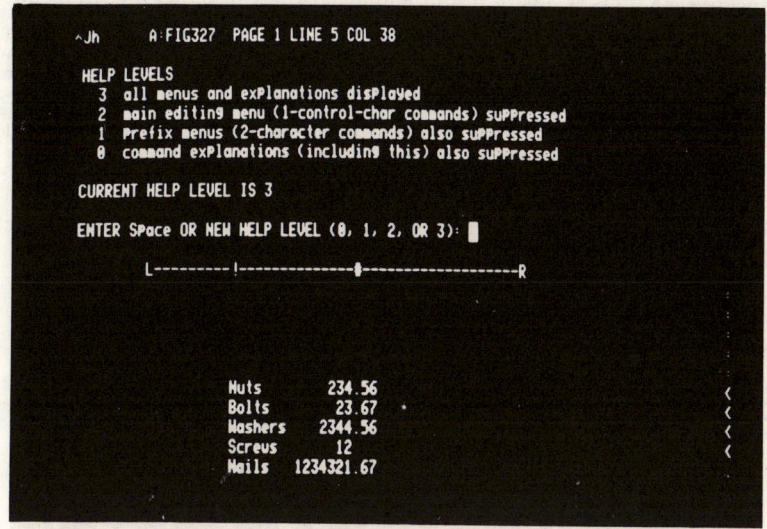

Fig 3.30 *display on help level 2*

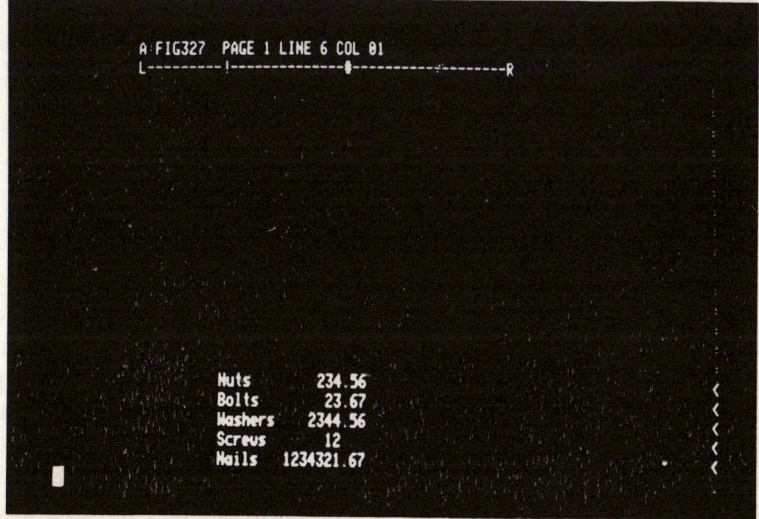

The 'O' menu is one which helps with the formatting of the text on the screen, and hence on the printed page. ^OL, ^OR, ^OI and ^ON we have already seen. ^OS is a very useful command since it allows text to be displayed with from one to nine spaces between the lines. ^OG allows you to set a paragraph tab so that although the cursor is at the extreme left-hand edge of the screen the next character to be typed appears indented for the start of a paragraph. To indent further press 'control O' and G again. You release the paragraph indent by pressing the RETURN key. ^OC typed after some text will centre it in order to provide, for example, a heading. See Figures 3.31 and 3.32 which demonstrate the layout before and after pressing ^OC.

Fig 3.31 *screen layout before pressing ^OC*

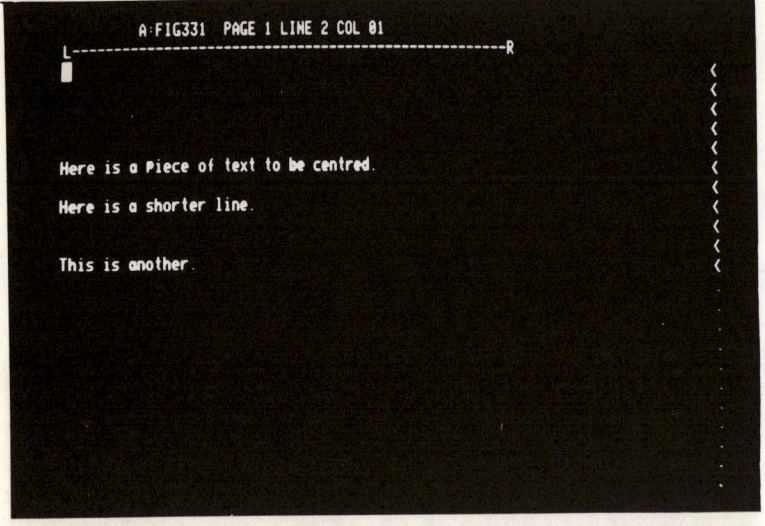

Another menu you will have had displayed to you earlier is the 'K' menu. This one is concerned with manipulating blocks of text. We have seen already that ^KD and ^KS will save text for us on disk. But there is far more than that available. It is most useful for us to be able to mark the beginning and end of blocks of text. Then we can do a large variety of things from that point. Let us first mark the start of a section of text. We do this by placing the cursor on the first character of the block and pressing 'control K' and B (see Figure 3.33). Then move the cursor to the end of the block we want to mark and press 'control K' and K. Then the entire

Fig 3.32 *screen layout after pressing ^OC*

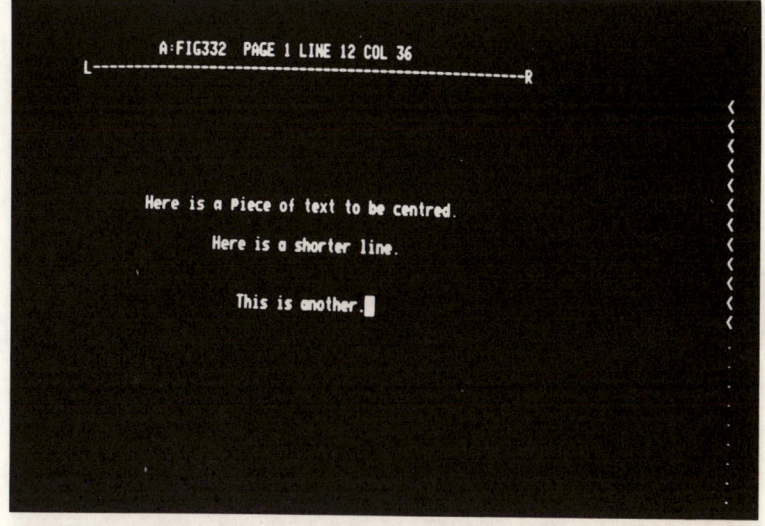

Fig 3.33 *marking a section of text*

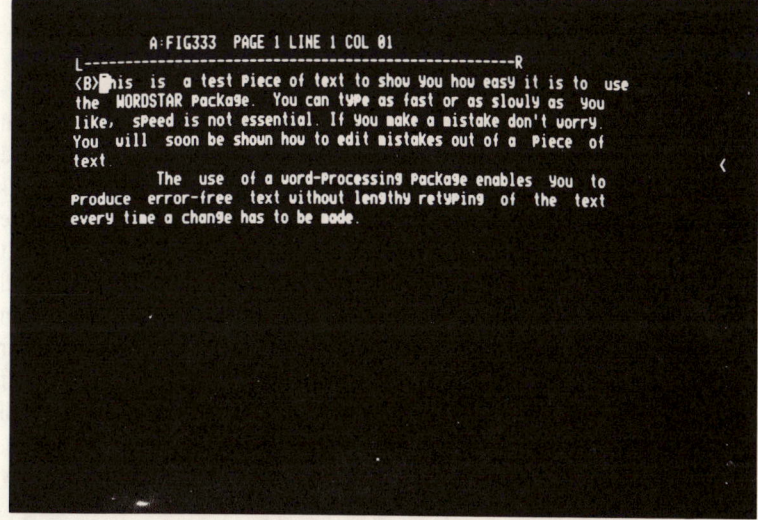

block is highlighted, as Figure 3.34 shows. We can then do a number of things with that block:

1. Copy the block to another part of the text (^KC).
2. Move the block to another part of the text (^KV).
3. Copy the block out to another file (^KW).
4. Delete the entire block (^KY).

Fig 3.34 *the block of text 'highlighted'*

Type in the following text:

Much of the power of computers is going to be placed at the disposal of people who work in offices. By the use of facilities such as word processing it is possible to eliminate much of the boring repetitious copy typing which is now done. In addition there is going to be the facility of having a cluster of computers connected together in what is called a 'local area network'. This means that the computers all have common access to files of data and printing facilities. It is then only a short step to having the computers connected together over telephone lines. This means that many executives only need visit their office infrequently as they will have direct connection to all the data they require from their home, where they will have a computer terminal from which they will be able to conduct the majority of their business.

Now move the cursor to the position shown in Figure 3.35, over the 'and' of 'and printing facilities. ', then type 'control K' followed by B. Then move the cursor until it is over the full stop at the end of the phrase. Finally move the cursor until it is over the space in front of the phrase

Fig **3.35** *moving a phrase within text*

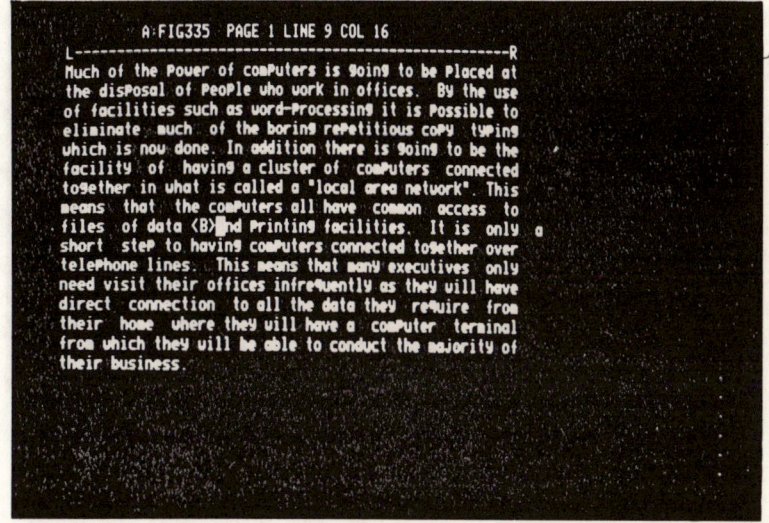

'they require from' and press 'control K' and V. The result should be as shown in Figure 3.36. You have moved the phrase 'and printing facilities' to another part of the text. If you want to copy the marked block to another part of the text you would type the ^KC command. To delete the whole block from your document – but remember it is lost for ever – you type the ^KY command. If you wanted to save a vital section of the text on to a disk file you type the ^KW command and you get the screen query as shown in Figure 3.37.

The last menu to deal with is the 'P' menu which controls the way text is presented when printed out. Using 'control P' before striking certain keys allows us to instruct the printer to underline text, print it in heavy type, print sub- and super-scripts and many other features. For instance, if you want a heading to be in heavy type then you place the cursor in front the first character you want emphasising and press 'control P' and follow this with B. At the end of the enhanced text you repeat the process so that you have 'bracketed' the text with a ^B character at each end. This tells Wordstar when to switch on the enhanced printing instructions and when to switch them off. You will get the text looking as shown in Figure 3.38. If you want to underline a piece of text you do the same as for

Fig 3.36 *moving the phrase completed*

```
            A:FIG335  PAGE 1 LINE 13 COL 36
L---------------------------------------------------R
Much of the power of computers is going to be placed at
the disposal of people who work in offices.  By the use
of facilities such as word-processing it is possible to
eliminate much of the boring repetitious copy typing
which is now done. In addition there is going to be the
facility  of  having a cluster of computers  connected
together in what is called a "local area network". This
means  that  the computers all have  common  access  to
files  of data .  It is  only  a
short  step to having computers connected together over
telephone lines.  This means that many executives  only
need visit their offices infrequently as they will have
direct  connection  to all the data<B>and printing facilities<K>  they   require +
their  home  where  they will have a computer  terminal
from which they will be able to conduct the majority of
their business.
```

Fig 3.37 *saving the text to disk*

```
^KW       A:FIG335  PAGE 1 LINE 16 COL 28

 ^S=delete character   ^Y=delete entry   ^F=File directory
 ^D=restore character  ^R=Restore entry  ^U=cancel command

    NAME OF FILE TO WRITE MARKED TEXT ON? █

L---------------------------------------------------R
together in what is called a "local area network". This
means  that  the computers all have  common  access  to
files  of  data .  It is only a short  step  to  having
computers connected together over telephone lines. This
means  that  many executives only  need  visit  their
offices  infrequently  as  they will  have.  direct
connection  to all the data<B>and printing facilities<K> they
require  from their home where they will have a computer
terminal  from which they will be able to  conduct  the
majority of their business.
```

Fig 3.38   *printing in heavy type using 'control P'*

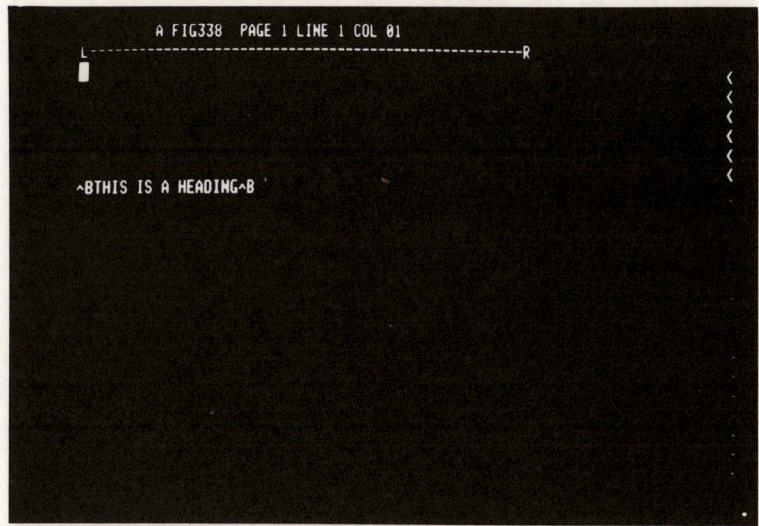

enhancing the printing but use ^PS before and after the text. Should you want to both enhance and underline you use both commands, as shown in Figure 3.39. But remember, you must press 'control P' before each command.

Fig 3.39   *enhanced and underlined text*

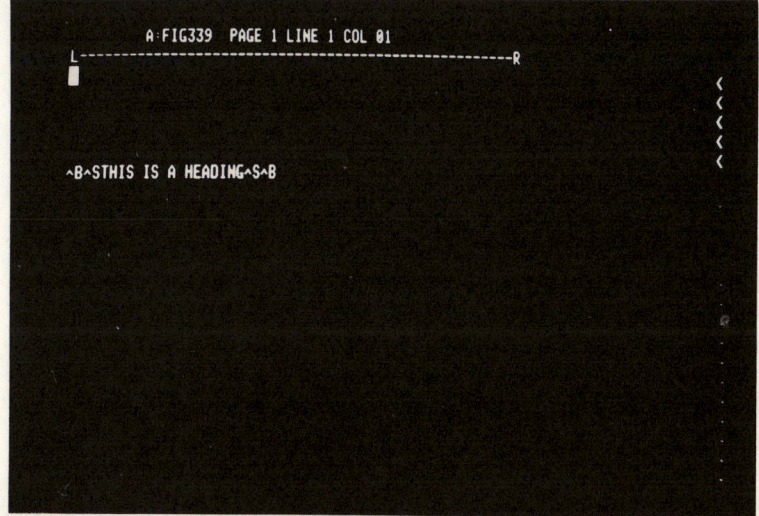

As the ^P commands take up space across the text they can play havoc with your spacing. However, you can switch them off and conceal them by pressing 'control O' followed by D. Then you see no print commands displayed. By repeating this command you return the control codes to the display. Try this and see. Some of the other commands in the 'P' menu will only work on certain printers, so try them out and see if they work for you. You should be able to print out lines such as:

$$Y = X^3 - 3X^2 + 4X + 2$$

without a lot of difficulty. The screen display for this will look as shown in Figure 3.40.

Fig 3.40 *screen display for equation*

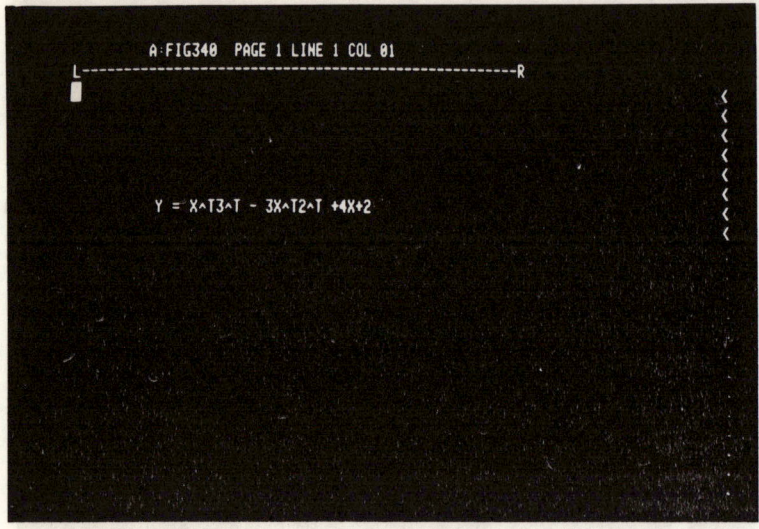

3.4 CONTROLLING THE OUTPUT

Wordstar provides a number of ways of controlling the output. Some of these are provided by the 'dot' commands. These are commands placed in strategic positions in the text and control such things as the length of the page, the top and bottom margins, headings and footings. For example, if we want to specify that the page length of our document is 9 lines, as we would if we were printing name and address labels, then '.PL9' at the head of the document would do that. To cause the printer to 'throw' a fresh page we would place '.PA' at the appropriate spot in the document. Top and bottom margins are specified by '.MT' and '.MB' followed by a number which indicates how many lines are to be left at the top and bottom. '.OP' tells Wordstar to omit the printing of page numbers at the bottom of each page – useful if you are writing single page letters. If you look at Figure 3.41 you will see commands used to create headings and

Fig 3.41 *commands for headings and footings*

```
.HE^K                          MASTERING WORDSTAR
.FO^K                                           #
.OP
```

footings for the manuscript of this book. .HE^K indicates that what follows is a heading text and that it is to be printed on the right-hand side of odd-numbered pages and the left-hand side of even-numbered pages. .FO^K is a footing command and states that at the bottom of each page there is to be a number, in the position marked by the # sign, again on the right of odd-numbered pages and the left of even-numbered pages. The .OP command turns off the usual page numbering at the centre of the bottom line of each page.

We can also control printing by using the 'mail–merge' feature available as an optional extra to Wordstar. This enables files to be merged together at print time so that name and address labels and personalised letters can be printed from a common name and address file. For example, if the name and address file contained the following:

Agnew, Mr., A. J., 14 Meadow Bank Road, READING, Berks,, RG20 4XT, 0256 34213
Blake, Mrs, L., "The Limes", Crown Lane, CAMBRIDGE, Cambs, CB3 3RT, 0223 21245
Cooper, Miss, A., 12 Wilkinson Cres., HUNTINGDON, Cambs,, PE19 1DF, 0480 6754

you will see that each of the lines contains nine fields of data separated by commas – one these fields can be blank as you can see in the first and the third lines. What we need now is a set of instructions which will extract the appropriate data, line by line, from the file and print it in a specified way. For example, look at Figure 3.42. The first line of this tells mail-merge (note the M at the end of the line) that the data is to be taken from a file called 'ADDRESS'. The next line tells Wordstar that the row of variables are to be called:

NAME, TITLE, INITS, ADDR1, ADDR2, ADDR4, PC, NO

These nine variable names exactly match the variables held on each row of the file. .OP switches off page numbering as we are going to print name and address labels on sticky labels which are provided on a continuous strip just 9 printer lines deep. Hence the instruction .PL9 specifying the page length of 9 lines. The .PO10 instructs that the printing is to be offset

Fig 3.42 *mail-merge feature display*

```
            ┤ FIG342   PAGE 1 LINE 1 COL 01
L --------------------------------------------------------R
■DF ADDRESS                                                          M
 RV NAME,TITLE,INITS,ADDR1,ADDR2,ADDR3,ADDR4,PC,NO                   M
 OP                                                                  <
 PL9                                                                 <
 PO10                                                                <
 MTO                                                                 <
 MBO                                                                 <
                                                                     <
 &TITLE& &INITS&&NAME&,                                              <
 &ADDR1&,                                                            <
 &ADDR2&,                                                            <
 &ADDR3&,                                                            <
 &ADDR4&,                                                            <
 &PC&,                                                               <
  PA                                                                 <
 --------------------------------------------------------------------P
```

10 columns. This is because of the layout requirement on the label – we don't want the name and address crowded to the left of the label. No top and bottom margins are required so we specify .MTO and .MBO. Then the layout of the text on the label is specified and we state the relative positions of each variable from each line of the file by enclosing the variable names in ampersands (& characters). The output when run, that is, when we call for the M (mail-merge) option, it looks as shown in Figure 3.43.

Fig 3.43 *output of mail-merge*

```
                    Mr. A.J.0256 34213
                    14 Meadow Bank Road
                    READING
                    Berks

                    RG20 4XT


                    Mrs L.0223 21245
                    The Limes
                    Crown Lane
                    CAMBRIDGE
                    Cambs
                    CB3 3RT
```

Fig **3.43** *continued*

```
           Miss A.0480 6754
           12 Wilkinson Cres.
           HUNTINGDON
           Cambs

           PE19 1DF
```

The sticky labels can then be peeled off and stuck on to envelopes which contain personalised letters with information taken from the same file. A sample letter is shown in Figure 3.44 with the results of printing the letter to the three people on the file shown in Figure 3.45. Another output from the same file is directed by the 'skeleton' letter shown in Figure 3.46 with the output shown in Figure 3.47.

Fig **3.44** *sample letter*

```
.DF ADDRESS
.RV NAME,TITLE,INITS,ADDR1,ADDR2,ADDR3,ADDR4,PC,PHONE
.OP

5th October 1984

&TITLE& &INITS& &NAME&,
&ADDR1&,
&ADDR2&,
&ADDR3&,
&ADDR4&

Dear &TITLE& &NAME&,

I  should like to inform you of our fabulous new offer which
is  available  to you, &TITLE&  &NAME&,  only.  Won't  your
friends  in &ADDR2& be envious of you when you drive  up  in
your  new 1985 THUNDERER sports car.  All you have to do  is
answer the six simple questions on the attached form and the
chance, &TITLE& &NAME& is yours.


Best wishes and good luck.


SPARKELWITE TOOTHPASTE COMPANY
```

Fig 3.45 *sample letter personalised for different names and addresses*

* * *

5th October 1984

Mr. A.J. Agnew,
14 Meadow Bank Road,
READING,
Berks,

Dear Mr. Agnew,

I should like to inform you of our fabulous new offer which
is available to you, Mr. Agnew, only. Won't your friends in
READING be envious of you when you drive up in your new 1985
THUNDERER sports car. All you have to do is answer the six
simple questions on the attached form and the chance, Mr.
Agnew is yours.

Best wishes and good luck.

SPARKELWITE TOOTHPASTE COMPANY

* * *

* * *

5th October 1984

Mrs L. Blake,
The Limes,
Crown Lane,
CAMBRIDGE,
Cambs

Dear Mrs Blake,

I should like to inform you of our fabulous new offer which
is available to you, Mrs Blake, only. Won't your friends in
Crown Lane be envious of you when you drive up in your new
1985 THUNDERER sports car. All you have to do is answer the
six simple questions on the attached form and the chance,
Mrs Blake is yours.

Best wishes and good luck.

SPARKELWITE TOOTHPASTE COMPANY

* * *

Fig 3.45 continued

* * *

5th October 1984

Miss A. Cooper,
12 Wilkinson Cres.,
HUNTINGDON,
Cambs,

Dear Miss Cooper,

I should like to inform you of our fabulous new offer which
is available to you, Miss Cooper, only. Won't your friends
in HUNTINGDON be envious of you when you drive up in your
new 1985 THUNDERER sports car. All you have to do is answer
the six simple questions on the attached form and the
chance, Miss Cooper is yours.

Best wishes and good luck.

SPARKELWITE TOOTHPASTE COMPANY

* * *

Fig 3.46 *'skeleton' letter*

```
.DF ADDRESS
.RV NAME,TITLE,INITS,ADDR1,ADDR2,ADDR3,ADDR4,PC,NO
.OP
.PL3
.PO10
.MT0
.MB0

&TITLE& &INITS&&NAME&,Telephone:-&NO&
.pa
```

Fig 3.47 *output of names and telephone numbers from previous
'skeleton'*

```
      Mr. A.J.Agnew,Telephone:-0256 34213


      Mrs L.Blake,Telephone:-0223 21245


      Miss A.Cooper,Telephone:-0480 6754
```

Wordstar is a very powerful screen-orientated word-processing package. Help with using its large number of commands can be obtained from its selection of menus. Page layout is clearly shown on the screen as the creation of a document proceeds. Documents have to be saved on disk before they can be printed. It has one advantage in that a very long document can be created but with only the section currently being edited in memory at any time. This tends to slow down the editing function as sections of text are swapped in and out of memory. It can also be rather frustrating waiting for Wordstar to move the cursor from the start to the finish of a long text. Searching and replacement can be done for phrases as well as single words. The mail–merge facility is very flexible and powerful.

3.5 INDEX OF WORDSTAR(TM) commands

^A	Cursor left word
^B	Reform paragraph
^C	Scroll up screen
^D	Cursor right character
^E	Cursor up one line
^F	Cursor right one word
^G	Delete one character to right
^H	Cursor left one character
^I	Tab
^J	HELP prefix
^K	BLOCK prefix
^L	Find/replace again
^M	RETURN
^N	Insert hard carriage return
^O	ON-SCREEN formatting prefix
^P	PRINT control prefix
^Q	EDITING prefix
^R	Scroll down screen
^S	Cursor left one character
^T	Delete word to the right
^U	Interrupt
^V	Insert on/off
^W	Scroll down one line
^X	Cursor down one line
^Y	Delete entire line
^Z	Scroll up one line
^JB	Explain re-forming
^JD	Explain printing directives

^JF	Explain Flags
^JH	Set Help level
^JI	Command index
^JM	Explain tabs & margins
^JP	Explain Place markers
^JR	Explain Ruler line
^JS	Explain Status line
^JV	Explain moVing text

^K0/^K9	Set/Hide markers
^KB	Mark/Hide block start
^KC	Copy block
^KD	Done edit
^KE	rEname file
^KF	File directory on/off
^KH	Hide/Display marked block
^KJ	Delete additional file
^KK	Mark blocK end
^KL	Change Logged disk
^KO	cOpy file
^KP	Print
^KQ	Quit edit
^KR	Read additional file
^KS	Save and re-edit
^KV	MoVe block
^KW	Write block to file
^KX	Save and eXit
^KY	Delete block

^OC	Centre text
^OD	Print control display on/off
^OE	Soft hyphen Entry on/off
^OF	Read margins & tabs from line
^OG	ParaGraph tab
^OH	Hyphen help on/off
^OI	Set tab stop
^OJ	Justification on/off
^OL	Set left margin
^ON	Clear tab stop
^OP	Page break on/off
^OR	Set right margin
^OS	Set line spacing
^OT	Ruler display on/off
^OW	Word wrap

^PA/^PZ   Enter print control characters ^A/^Z
^PM   Make next line overprint
^PO   Enter non-break space

^QO/^Q9   Cursor to markers 0/9
^QA   Find & replace
^QB   Cursor to Block start
^QC   Cursor to end of file
^QD   Cursor to right enD of line
^QE   Cursor to top of screen
^QF   Find
^QK   Cursor to block end
^QP   Cursor to Previous position
^QQ   Repeat next command
^QR   Cursor to staRt of file
^QS   Cursor to Start of line
^QV   Cursor source*
^QW   Continuous down scroll
^QX   Cursor to bottom of screen
^QY   Delete to end of line
^QZ   Continuous downward scroll
^Qdel   Delete to beginning of line

*This means that the cursor is either restored to its position before the last ^QA command or to its position at the source of the last block moved, copied or deleted.

APPLEWRITER

4.1 INTRODUCTION APPLEWRITER II

This text was prepared using an Apple IIe microcomputer and readers should note that slight variations are noticeable between this and Applewriter as set up for other computers in the range.

Getting used to Applewriter means one needs to become acquainted with some of the peculiarities of the Apple keyboard first of all. Some of the keys are in slightly unusual positions and there are two keys specific to the machine itself. These are known as 'open-Apple' and 'solid-Apple', after the pictograms engraved on the keys. The keys are situated on either side of the spacebar at the bottom of the keyboard, as shown in Figure 4.1.

Fig 4.1 *keyboard of Applewriter IIe*

Starting Applewriter from scratch is simple. The master disk is inserted into the main drive, 'Drive 1' in Apple-speak, and the computer is switched on. The drive motor starts up and before long the sign-on display comes up on the screen. This is shown in Figure 4.2 and it can be seen that this word processor is similar to Wordstar in that it is said to be **menu driven**. The menus can be listed by pressing the 'open Apple' key together with the ? symbol. The selection of menus is then presented as shown in Figure 4

Fig 4.2 *sign-on display*

```
            Apple Writer //
       Copyright 1981-2, Paul Lutus
     Copyright 1981-2, Apple Computer Inc
```

For HELP while editing,
press open-Apple and "?")
Press RETURN :█

Fig 4.3 *selection of menus on Applewriter*

```
            HELP SCREEN MENU
        A. Command Summary
        B. Cursor Movement
        C. Upper/Lower Case Change
        D. Delete/Retrieve Text
        E. Tabs
        F. Glossary
        G. Saving Files
        H. Loading Files
        I. Find/Replace Text
        J. Embedded Print Commands

        Press RETURN to Exit
        Enter Your Selection (A - J) :█
```

Instructions on how to obtain each menu are simply displayed and it can be seen that the commands are given by very simple key strokes. In fact, Applewriter allows the user to get down very quickly to creating new text.

Having started Applewriter and arrived at the start-up display all you do is to press the RETURN key and an almost blank screen is presented to you; at the top you will find a status line, similar to those presented by most other word-processing packages. Type in your text and away you go! Try typing in the following:

It is very simple to get started using this word-processing package. The keys are arranged in a very similar manner to those of a type-writer and as with all the others described in this book you do not have to press the RETURN key at the end of every line. The text automatically 'wraps round' as you type it in. Justification in this word processor takes place at the time of printing, as does the setting of the margins.

The text will now look as shown in Figure 4.4. How to print it within various margins will be dealt with later.

In order to move around the text you have already typed in you can use the arrow keys which are situated at the bottom of the keyboard on

Fig 4.4 *sample of text on Applewriter*

```
It is very simple to get started using this word-processing package. The keys
are arranged in a very similar manner to those of a typewriter and as with all
the others described in this book you do not have to press the RETURN key at
the end of every line. The text automatically "wraps round" as you type it in.
Justification in this word-processor takes place at the time of printing as
does the setting of the margins.
```

the right. When pressed, these keys allow you to move around the text either up and down one line at a time, or left and right one character at a time. If the arrow keys are pressed in conjunction with the 'solid-Apple' key then vertical movement is made twelve lines at a time and horizontal movement one word at a time. To get to the beginning of the text you have to press CONTROL – B and to get to the end you press CONTROL – E. Note that all the CONTROL key commands are shown in the manual as, for example, [B] for CONTROL – B or [E] for CONTROL – E.

Deleting characters is very simple. To delete a single character use the DELETE key. This will delete the character to the left of the cursor. If the 'open-Apple' key is used in conjunction with the left and right arrow keys you can delete characters with the first operation and restore them to the text with the second! To delete whole words press CONTROL – D and follow this with CONTROL – W. But more of these later. The operations, and other deletion operations are listed in the menu shown Figure 4.5. Not all the operations listed in this menu are immediately obvious, but they will be explained later on. Any of the available menus can be displayed by pressing 'open-Apple' followed by '?' and the menus will replace the displayed text. This does not mean that your text has been lost. It is preserved in memory until you return from the menus. Then you can carry on with your typing as if nothing had happened.

Insertion of new text into existing text is very simple. All that has to be done is to place the cursor, using the arrow keys, at the start of the passage to be inserted and you can start typing. The text to the right of the cursor merely moves over to accommodate the new text as each character is typed in. Try this by inserting the additional text below into the text you have already produced, shown in Figure 4.4.

> The deletion of text is also very easy. You can delete single characters by using the DEL key, or if you are frightened that you might delete characters by mistake you can use the 'open-Apple' and arrow keys to delete characters and restore them if need be.

78

Fig 4.5 *delete/retrieve menu*

```
        APPLE WRITER // COMMAND SUMMARY            PAGE 4
------------------------------------------------------------------
                        DELETE/RETRIEVE
COMMAND/KEYSTROKE            ACTION
-----------------       ------------------------------------------

OPEN-APPLE LEFT-ARROW   DELETES 1 character to left of cursor
OPEN-APPLE RIGHT-ARROW  RETRIEVES 1 character at cursor
DELETE key              DELETES text to left of cursor - cannot retrieve

Set data line arrow to < by [D]
     [W]                DELETES 1 word  to left of cursor
     [X]                DELETES paragraph or 1024 characters to left of cursor

     SOLID-APPLE with
     [W]                COPIES a word to buffer
     [X]                COPIES a paragraph to buffer

Set data line arrow to > by [D]
     [W]                RETRIEVES 1 word at cursor
     [X]                RETRIEVES 1 paragraph or 1024 characters at cursor

 Press "C" to continue, or "E" to Exit, and then press RETURN ▌
```

The new text then will look as shown in Figure 4.6.

To print text which is in memory all that has to be done is to press CONTROL - P. Remember that is shown as P enclosed in heavy square brackets in the menus of commands, at which point the printing prompt appears at the bottom of the screen. If you respond with 'NP' then printing commences.

Fig 4.6 *insertion of additonal text*

```
It is very simple to get started using this word-processing package. The keys
are arranged in a very similar manner to those of a typewriter and as with all
the others described in this book you do not have to press the RETURN key at
the end of every line. The text automatically "wraps round" as you type it in.
The deletion of text is also very easy. You can delete single characters by
using the DEL key or, if you are frightened that you might delete characters by
mistake you can use the "open-Apple" and arrow keys to delete characters and
restore them if need be. Justification in this word-processor takes place at
the time of printing as does the setting of the margins.▌
```

There are more printing commands and also a way of embedding printing instructions within a piece of text. These will be dealt with later on.

Having prepared a piece of text and dealt with any necessary editing or entering, the text can be saved away on disk. This is done by pressing CONTROL - S and responding with the name you wish to give the saved file, followed by D1 or D2, depending on which drive will stored the file. This means that:

MYTEXT,D2

will save the file called 'MYTEXT' on Drive 2.

4.2 APPLEWRITER MENUS

The menus which are available for the Applewriter are obtained, as has been explained previously, by pressing 'open-Apple' and '?'. For the special 'print command' menu press CONTROL - P and follow that by the '?' symbol. This then produces the menu shown in Figure 4.7. The

Fig 4.7 *print command menu*

```
Print/Program Commands:

Left       Margin    (LM) = 0
Paragraph  Margin    (PM) = 0
Right      Margin    (RM) = 79
Top        Margin    (TM) = 1
Bottom     Margin    (BM) = 1
Page Number          (PN) = 1
Printed Lines        (PL) = 58
Page Interval        (PI) = 66
Line Interval        (LI) = 0
Single Page          (SP) = 0
Print Destination    (PD) = 1
Carriage Return      (CR) = 0
Underline Token      (UT) = \
Print Mode (LJ,FJ,CJ,RJ) = LJ
Top Line             (TL) :

Bottom Line          (BL) :

Press RETURN to Exit

[P]rint/Program :█
```

data shown gives the current specification for text that is to be printed. All the entries are called 'default' values and are values wich are set up automatically when Applewriter is loaded. They can be very easily changed by typing the code letters followed by the relevant instructions. For example to set the margins to be in columns 10 and 64 respectively one types 1m10 and rm64 so that these values appear in the data table to replace the existing entries.

The TL and BL commands are those which control printing at the top and bottom of each page. There are three parts to each of these. They consist of what is printed on the left of the page, in the middle of the page and on the right of the page. Each part is separated by an asterisk (*) so that if we type:

TL*Mastering Applewriter*Chapter 1*£*

we will have printed across the top of every page the words 'Mastering Applewriter' on the left, 'Chapter 1' in the middle and the page number on the right.

Similarly, if we type:

BL**£**

we will get nothing printed on the left of the last line of the page, the page number in the centre and nothing at the right-hand end of that bottom line. The '*' characters serve to separate the left, centre and right elements of the top and bottom lines of the page.

It must be remembered however, that these controls must be placed in the data table before printing takes place. They are lost when the computer is switched off. There are ways of preserving printing formats and these will be described later on.

The page number (PN) command tells Applewriter the number of the first page to be printed when this particular piece of text comes to be printed.

A peculiarity of Applewriter is that when it is printing a document which has a bottom-line instruction operative you must end the text with the form-feed instruction. ff, which will cause the printer to jump to the end of the current page when the printing is finished. This means that it will print the bottom line, which usually contains the page number, for the last page as well as for all the other pages, otherwise the bottom line of the last page of the document will not be printed.

One of the menus available is that which tells you what the embedded print commands will offer you. It is shown in Figure 4.8, and is reached by pressing 'j' while in the menu shown in Figure 4.3. From this you will see that you can include print commands in the text, **embedded commands**, which, like those in a number of the other word-processing packages, are prefixed by a dot. For example, .LM10 will set the left margin in the 10th column and .RM40 will set the right margin at column 40:

```
So  that any text which is  now
printed  will  be  set  between
those  margins and will  appear
like this.
```

In order to reset the margins back to where they were the commands, for example,

Fig 4.8 *embedded print command menu*

```
                        APPLE WRITER // COMMAND SUMMARY            PAGE 10A
------------------------------------------------------------------------
                          EMBEDDED PRINT COMMANDS
COMMAND/KEYSTROKE                    ACTION
----------------                 ---------------------------------------
[P] ?        Accesses PRINT/PROGRAM COMMANDS menu
[P] np       PRINTS present file to screen or printer

\phrase\     UNDERLINES all characters between backslashes
.UTx         Defines Underline Token to be "x"

.LM£         Sets LEFT margin at character space £
.RM£         Sets RIGHT margin at character space £
.LM+or-£     Adds or subtracts from left margin setting by £
.RM+or-£     Adds or subtracts from right margin setting by £
.PM+or-£     Indents/outdents 1st line of paragraph by +or-£
.EP0         Printer ignores all text following
.EP1         Printer prints all text following

    ALL EMBEDDED PRINT COMMANDS MUST BE ON LINES BY THEMSELVES
    except UNDERLINE

Press "C" to continue, or "E" to Exit, and then press RETURN ▮
```

    .LM9
    .RM64

will do the trick.

Alternatively, if one needs to set paragraphs in from the left-hand or right-hand margins, then they can be changed temporarily by the commands embedded in the text of:

    .LM+10
    .RM−20

which can then be reversed having entered the text as follows:

```
This is a paragraph which
is set in a separate block
by the dot commands which
have increased the left
margin by 10 and reduced
the right margin by 20.
the margins can then be
set back to where they
were by 'switching off'
the revised margins by
typing the 'opposite'
embedded commands:-
```

    .LM−10
    .RM+20

This type of command can also be used to indent the first line of a paragraph – or indeed to extend it if need be. For example if we put in the command:

.PM+20

We will cause this paragraph to have the same right margin as before but the first line set in by 20 characters from the left margin, while all subsequent lines are kept at the original left margin.

.PM−5

```
The  above  embedded printing command will  set the
     first  line of this paragraph five  characters
     to the left of the rest of the paragraph.
```

In order to retain a printer control table of the sort shown in Figure 4.7 without having to reset it every time a particular document is printed we can save the table by using the command CONTROL – Q followed by D. This comes from the menu shown in Figure 4.9. This is the additional functions menu. From this you can see that you can load in the previously saved printer control table by CONTROL – Q followed by C, thus saving you the task of redefining the printing layout each time you print the document.

Fig 4.9 *additional functions menu*

```
            ADDITIONAL FUNCTIONS MENU

        A. Load Tab File
        B. Save Tab File
        C. Load Print/Program Value File
        D. Save Print/Program Value File
        E. Load [G]lossary File
        F. Save [G]lossary File
        G. Toggle Carriage Return Display
        H. Toggle Data Line Display
        I. Connect Keyboard to Printer
        J. Convert Apple Writer 1.1 Files
        K. Quit Apple Writer

        Press RETURN to Exit

        Enter your selection (A - K) :█
```

Another menu is that which tells you all about how sections of the text are found by Applewriter and manipulated in various ways. This is shown in Figure 4.10 – reached by pressing I after getting into the main help menu as shown in Figure 4.3.

We can demonstrate the find/replace function using this paragraph. To do this we use the CONTROL – F command followed by the necessary detailed instructions. But before we do this let us show how a piece of text can be copied from one part of the document to another. This is done by positioning the cursor at the start of the text and saving it. This is done by pressing CONTROL – S and following the name under which it is to be saved by an identification of the end of the text sandwiched between ! symbols. Like this:

        para!this:–!,d2

This saves the defined text on drive 2 under the name of 'para'.

Fig 4.10 *find/replace text menu*

```
              APPLE WRITER // COMMAND SUMMARY              PAGE 9
---------------------------------------------------------------------
                        FIND/REPLACE TEXT
COMMAND/KEYSTROKE                ACTION
-----------------               -------------------------------------
   SEARCHES FROM CURSOR POSITION IN DIRECTION OF DATA LINE ARROW

[F]/text/                FINDS text

[F]/old text/new text/   FINDS old text, replaces with new text.
                         (Asks for confirmation)

[F]/old text/new text/a  FINDS old text, replaces with new text
                         (All occurrences)

[F]/text//               FINDS text and deletes it
[F]=                     Repeats previous FIND command

Press "C" to continue, or "E" to Exit, and then press RETURN ▮
```

Then move the cursor to the position when the copied text is to be inserted and then the saved paragraph is loaded by typing CONTROL – L followed by:

        para,d2

and the previously saved paragraph reappears in its new position.

We can demonstrate the find/replace function using this paragraph. To do this we use the CONTROL – F command followed by the necessary detailed instructions. But before we do this let us show how a piece of text can be copied from one part of the document to another. This is done by positioning the cursor at the start of the text and saving it. This is done by pressing CONTROL – S and following the name under which it is to be saved by an identification of the end of the text sandwiched between ! symbols. Like this:

CONTROL – F allows us to find a piece of text and replace it with another piece of text. You press CONTROL – F and reply with, say,

    /text/document/

if we are to replace the word 'text' by the word 'document' in the above paragraph, and the result is shown below:

We can demonstrate the find/replace function using this paragraph. To do this we use the CONTROL – F command followed by the necessary detailed instructions. But before we do this let us show how a piece of document can be copied from one part of the document to another. This is done by positioning the cursor at the start of the document and saving it. This is done by pressing CONTROL – S and following the name under which it is to be saved by an identification of the end of the document sandwiched between ! symbols. Like this:

What happens is that every time Applewriter finds the word 'text' it asks you first of all whether you want the replacement to take place; it then awaits your answer, Y or N. After that you are asked if you want to proceed. This you do by pressing RETURN. The thing you have to watch in the replacement of text is the direction of the arrow in the top left-hand corner of the screen. If it points to the right ($>$) then the search will take place forwards through the document. If it faces left ($<$) then the search takes place backwards through the document. The direction of the arrow is controlled by CONTROL – D which acts as a 'toggle' switching the arrow between its two directions.

Complete words, and paragraphs if necessary , can be deleted by use of the CONTROL – W and CONTROL – X commands. In order to delete a word we place the cursor after the last character of the word to be deleted and then press CONTROL – D. Applewriter will then delete all the characters to the left of the cursor up to the space preceding those characters, provided that the arrow (remember CONTROL (– D) points to the left. If you find that you have by accident deleted the wrong word you can retrieve it by setting the arrow to point to the right and pressing CONTROL – W again. The same kind of technique is used to remove complete paragarphs. For the purposes of Applewriter a paragraph is any section of text terminated by the RETURN character. As the deletion of a paragraph works backwards, as with the deletion of a word, the end of one paragraph must be the beginning of another. Hence we must make sure that the arrow points to the left and position the cursor at the end of the paragraph to be deleted. Then we press CONTROL – X. The paragraph then disappears from the screen. To return the deleted paragraph we reverse the arrow and press CONTROL – X again and it reappears. Actually, if a paragraph contains more than 1024 characters then only 1024 characters are deleted. What Applewriter actually does is to search backwards from the cursor position until it finds a RETURN character and it deletes all the characters between the cursor and the RETURN. On the other hand, if it has searched through 1024 characters without finding a RETURN then it looks no further.

4.3 MORE ABOUT CONTROLLING TEXT

Controlling the look of the printed text by means of Applewriter commands is very simple. Text can be left-justified:

So that it looks like this

or right-justified

so that it looks like this

or we can centre-justify

so that it looks like this
or this
or even this

The normal layout for text, as it is in this book, is obtained by **fill-justifying** which is justifying at both the left-hand and right-hand margins. Each line contains complete words and the number of words and the spaces between them just fill a line. Applewriter supplies the addition spaces to make each line the same length. The LM and RM commands, mentioned in section 4.2 define the line length.

Left-justification only is obtained by embedding .LJ in the text like this:

.LJ

before the text which is required to be left-justified. Similarly right-justification is signalled by:

.RJ

Centre-justification by:

.CJ

and fill-justification by:

.FJ

Remember, however, that if you want to perform any of these functions then once they have served their purpose they have to be 'switched off' by means of another justification command since they stay in force until cancelled.

Because Applewriter displays everything on the screen as it is typed in the lines are all of a ragged length and there is no justification, centring or any layout of any kind. You will see that there is no indentation of paragraphs nor is there any page layout as you get with Wordstar, for example. It is important to see what your text is going to look like before printing takes place and this can be done by asking for print, but with the output directed to the screen rather than the printer. This is achieved by use of a 'switch' set by first pressing CONTROL – P, for printing to be initiated, but replying with PD=0, so we see

[P] rint:PD=0

on the screen. We then start printing off by pressing CONTROL – P again and responding with NP. The the text appears on the screen just as it would on the printed page. Set PD=1 and the text will appear at the printer. An example to illustrate this procedure is shown in Figures 4.11 and 4.12. Figure 4.11 shows what the raw text looks like and Figure 4.12 shows it when it is 'printed' on the screen.

Fig 4.11 *procedure for printing on-screen (1)*

```
.lj
This is left justified
.rj
This is right justified
.fj
.lm15
.rm70
.pm+5
This has had the paragraph format set up so that we get indenting. Then we have
to take off the paragraph command with .pm0
.pm0
So that the paragraphing no longer happens.█
```

Fig 4.12 *procedure for printing on-screen (2)*

```
Print Destination    (PD) = 0
Carriage Return      (CR) = 0
Underline Token      (UT) = \
Print Mode (LJ,FJ,CJ,RJ) = LJ
Top Line             (TL) :

Bottom Line          (BL) :

Press RETURN to Exit

[P]rint/Program :NP


         This is a piece of demonstration text which contains
         embedded print commands.  This is a piece of
         demonstration text which contains embedded print
         commands
                   This piece of text is centred
         This is left justified

                                This is right justified
                 This has had the paragraph format set up so that
         we get indenting. Then we have to take off the
         paragraph command with .pm0
         So that the paragraphing no longer happens.
       (Press RETURN) ■
```

Applewriter provides you with nine tab stops set at every eighth position, but these are always measured from the beginning of the file and not from the edge of the screen as with other word processors. The status line at the top of the screen always tells you the position of the tab stop after the last entered RETURN character; this is, after the last time the RETURN key was pressed. CONTROL – T followed by S sets a tab at the current cursor position. CONTROL – T followed by C clears the tab at the current cursor position and CONTROL – T followed by P purges all tab stops. Tabbing actually takes place only on the line being entered and you cannot tab from one line to the next. Although this sounds quite complicated it turns out that the tabbing works in just the same way as with Wordstar or Wordcraft. CONTROL – I or the tab key tabs the cursor across to the required position. Once tabs have been set up along a line then they are available for subsequent lines. Three tab positions have been set up in order to create the following table:

Sally	Cambridge	Single
Jane	Wigan	Single
Susan	York	Married
Mary	Hastings	Divorced
Louise	Dover	Single

As with all word processors there is the facility to merge existing text with the current document in memory. The options offered by Applewriter are quite considerable in this area. For example, one can load in part of a file which is stored on disk. By typing CONTROL - L followed by the file name and the starting point and finishing point of the text to be merged we can select portions of the stored text to be brought into memory. For example, if the file stored away contained the sentence:

Now is the time for all good men to come to the aid of the party.

then we can load it in at the current cursor position by a command which on the screen looks like:

[L] oad:file1 ,d2/Now/party./

and the entire portion of text saved in the file called 'file1' between the word 'now' and the word 'party.' (note the inclusion of the full stop) will be copied from the file. The slashes separating the key words are called **delimiters**. Remember that [L] is obtained by pressing CONTROL - L.

If we had wanted to we could have said:

[L] oad:file1 ,d2/Now/

and we would have loaded everything from the word 'Now' to the end of the file 'file1' into memory.

Similarly, if we had said:

[L] oad:file1 ,d2//party./

then we would have had the entire text from 'file1' which could be quite considerable, up to and including the word 'party.'.

There are a number of useful variations on this theme which you will find in the Applewriter manual. One which will be used in the next section is the one where we say:

[L] oad:file1 ,d2/Now/party./N

which loads everything in as before *except* the starting and finishing words, so that only

is the time for all good men to come to the aid of the

is loaded.

One feature not found in the other word processors is the ability to append a piece of text to the end of one already saved on disk. Normally when a file is saved it replaces any file previously saved with the same name. In order to ease the tasks of loading a file, going to its end, typing in new text and then saving the new, larger, file you can create your text and then save it on the end of an existing file by typing:

[S] ave;filename,d2+

where 'filename' is the name of an existing file.

Another valuable feature is that of being able to 'preview' a file before loading it – very useful if you want to merge a file with existing text and you are not sure if you are going to load the correct one in. If you type:

[L] oad;filename,d2

and then follow this with the 'backslash' character you will have the file copied from disk on to the screen but not into memory. Your correct document in memory is not touched in any way and if you are satisfied that you have the file you want it then can be loaded properly into memory with the command shown above minus the backslash. If you want to load a file into a completely clear memory, in other words you do not want to have the loaded piece of text merged with the existing text, you must press CONTROL – N which will erase the current document from memory. Then you can load the new file in for editing.

If you wish to see what files there are saved away on disk you can type CONTROL – L followed by ? and the files will be listed out for you.

Finally we come to a feature of Applewriter which is really time-saving. It is that feature which allows us to enter one-line pieces of text, words which we constantly mis-spell or that we use very often, by a single keystroke.

The **glossary**, as it is called, is under the control of CONTROL – G. When these keys are pressed we get the message:

[G] lossary(?=Define/*=Purge):

If we respond with the ? sign – no RETURN is needed – we are asked to enter a new definition. If we then type in the key letter for the text and follow this by the text itself we enter this into the glossary. All that is then needed is to press CONTROL – G followed by the key letter of the text we want and the text if refers to is placed in the text. Whenever we define a new entry in the glossary we get a list of the current glossary entries displayed, so that we do not have to write them down.

Glossary files can be saved and loaded in a similar way to print output files. Figure 4.13 shows the contents of a file called GLOSSARY. To

Fig 4.13 *contents of a file called GLOSSARY*

```
aDear Sir
bYours sincerely
cYours faithfully
dWindmill Computing
e23 Walker Street
fHUNTINGDON
gCambs PE5 2QT
```

print out any entry in the glossary all that has to be done is to place the cursor at the place where the text is to begin and press CONTROL – G followed by the appropriate reference letter and the piece of text will appear in the right place. This is how the blank letter in Figure 4.14 was created.

Fig 4.14   *blank letter printed out from the glossary*

```
                              Windmill Computing
                              23 Walker Street
                              HUNTINGDON
                              Cambs PE5 2QT


Dear Sir




Yours faithfully
```

4.4 USING WPL

Applewriter provides you with a Word Processing Language – WPL – which enables you to write programs to manipulate text automatically. This it does by first of all allowing you to use all the CONTROL commands in a very simple programming language. For example, if you wanted to do a particular task regularly such as loading and printing out a certain document which would involve:

1. Clearing memory
2. Loading the document
3. Setting the cursor to the start of the document
4. Printing the document

You could write

    NY
    L DOCUMENT,D2

B
PNP

and then save the 'program' under the name, say, if 'printdoc'.

All you then have to do is to press CONTROL – P and respond with:

DO printdoc,d2

and the loading and printing is done automatically.

The first letter on each line stands for a CONTROL command; P for CONTROL – P, B for CONTROL – B and so on. The first line says 'clear the memory', since CONTROL – N will produce the prompt which asks you if you wish to clear out the contents of memory.

If you respond with 'Y' then the memory is cleared. So NY represents the control command and the response. The second line is the load instruction for which we normally have to type CONTROL – L and the appropriate file-name. In WPL we use L and supply the response. Next, the B̄ stands for the CONTROL – B command which sends the cursor to the top of the document just loaded. Finally PNP stands for the CONTROL – P command and the response 'NP' to start the printing off.

In order to print a series of letters with personalised addresses and salutations we first of all have to create a document file containing the names and addresses followed by the salutation in the example which follows. Part of the file is shown in Figure 4.15 and the file is called

Fig 4.15 *file called 'addresses'*

```
‡1‡Mr.G.Jones
14 Kings Walk
Stamford
PE9 2QS


Dear Mr Jones
‡2‡Miss S.Hay
22 Cheyne Walk
Chelmsford
CH2 3ER


Dear Sally
‡3‡Sir J.French
"Court Lodge"
Walmer KENT
DE3 6TY


Dear Sir John
‡4‡Mr.F.Taylor
34 Elm Road
Warton Salop
```

'addresses'. Notice that each address is prefixed with a number enclosed between asterisks. The asterisks are not important, they could be any type of left and right delimiter, and serve only to identify the individual record. These numbers are used in the WPL program which we will write. The letter which will go out to all the people on the mailing list is shown in Figure 4.16. Note that the space which will be occupied by the address and salutation is denoted by (Address).

Fig 4.16   *letter ready for personalisation*

```
.*5
*65
                        U.T.C.Trading Co.,Ltd.,
                        U.T.C.House,
                        Wharton,
                        Norfolk,
                        NR4 6QT


1st January 1984


(Address)

I am pleased to inform you that our new range of floppy discs and accessories
are now available. The latest price list is enclosed. As valued and regular
customers we are pleased to offer you special discounts on all purchases made
before the end of the current month.

Assuring you of our best attention at all times.
```

What the WPL program will do is to identify by its number the section of the address file which is required and then transfer it to the position defined by the marker shown above. We put all this into the WPL file called 'FORM' and then "DO" it.

The file called 'FORM' is shown in Figure 4.17. There are two things to notice about it. One is that the letters, L and P which stand for the load and print commands, must be at least one space in from the left-hand edge of the text. The second is that there are three 'labels', such as we have in certain computer programming languages. These labels are REPEAT, OK and STOP and represent parts of the program to which 'jumps' are made. If this is getting too much for people with no programming experience, do not worry, it does not get any more difficult than this! All you have to do is to remember that the instructions are carried out one after the other in sequence unless the sequence is broken by an instruction which says 'GO to an instruction with a particular label on it

Fig 4.17 *the file called FORM*

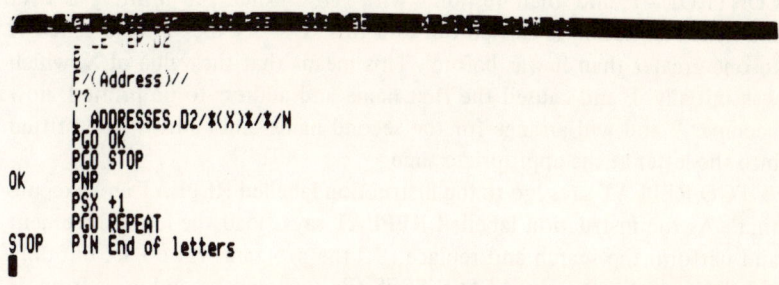

```
         LE  EP  DZ
         E
         F/(Address)//
         Y?
         L ADDRESSES,D2/*(X)*/*/N
         PGO OK
         PGO STOP
OK       PNP
         PSX +1
         PGO REPEAT
STOP     PIN End of letters
```

and carry on from there'. It is exactly the same as saying 'Go to jail, go directly to jail. Do not pass GO and do not collect £200!'.

Step-by-step, what is happening is basically this: the first of the program steps says 'set a variable called X to have the value 1' – that is what PSX 1 means.

The next step, 'NY' says 'clear the memory' and this instruction has the label REPEAT attached to it, so that at an appropriate point in the program a 'jump' is made to that instruction.

L LETTER,D2 means 'load the file called LETTER stored on drive D2'.

B means 'go to the start of the document now in memory.

F/(Address)// means 'find the piece of text between the first pair of slashes and replace it with a blank'.

Y? is the response which says 'perform the replacement and stop searching'.

The next step is to tell Applewriter to load that portion of the file called 'ADDRESSES' between the number enclosed between asterisks, initially 1, and the next asterisk. Remember that it is the N at the end of the command string which instructs that the beginning and end markers are not loaded. This ensures that all that part of the file which contains the first address and the first salutation is loaded into the document currently in memory at the current cursor position. Hence, the letter has a name, address and salutation dropped into the correct place and when the instruction to print the document is given that personalised letter will be printed.

PGO OK means 'the next instruction you carry out carries the OK label'.

'PGO STOP' is the instruction carried out if the next sequence of instructions cannot be carried out. If this is so the program jumps to the instruction labelled STOP. In order to understand this we have to see what happens when the next instruction carried out is that bearing the OK label.

The instruction labelled OK says 'PNP' and this means 'print the current document in memory' – it has the same effect as when we press CONTROL – P and then respond with 'NP'. When the printing is over the next instruction is carried out and this says 'set the variable called X to one greater than it was before'. This means that the value of X, which was initially 1 and caused the first name and address to be printed, now becomes 2 and will arrange for the second name and address to be fitted into the letter at the appropriate time.

PGO REPEAT says 'go to the instruction labelled REPEAT and execute that'. As the instruction labelled REPEAT says 'load the letter document and perform the search and replace . . .' the program will do so, but only if it has a section of the ADDRESSES file to draw the addresses from. If the list of addresses has been exhausted then Applewriter will recognise that fact and unless told to do otherwise – computers and programs are very stupid and will only do what they are told to do – will send out a cry for help! That cry for help is called an **Error message** and when an error message is sent to you, the user, it is up to you to do something about it. However, the WPL can trap it out by automatically sending the program to the line after the one which caused the error message to occur. In this case if the section of program labelled REPEAT causes an error then the line immediately after PGO OK is carried out.

PGO STOP means 'go to the instruction which is labelled STOP and do that. At that label, the last instruction in the program as it happens, is 'PIN end of letters'. This means 'Print the words "End of letters" on the screen'.

Now you have printed four letters all containing the same data and text but seemingly typed individually to the people on our file of addresses. This is only one example of the use to which the Applewriter WPL can be put. There are many more, some of them very sophisticated indeed.

Applewriter is very simple to use and since help menus are readily obtainable during the course of creating a document the manual is only really needed for extending one's knowledge of the system. WPL may frighten off the casual observer at first since it does require some idea of how a computer program is written. But it is easy to use once confidence is gained. The glossary facility is a boon both to bad spellers and to people who tend to have to use certain phrases a great deal. This could be of great value, for example, to those of us who have to type out scientific texts full of long, complicated words and expressions.

T/MAKER

5.1 INTRODUCING T/MAKER III

T/Maker III is a computer program which provides, as well as word processing, the facilities of a spreadsheet, graphical display of information, list-processing and a number of other useful features. These are all integrated in one program, but we are only going to look at the word processing function for the purposes of this book.

T/Maker runs on the CP/M operating system and again, being a program which runs on a general purpose microcomputer, uses various combinations of keys to carry out the editing process on a document.

To use T/Maker, first of all start up the CP/M operating system – **boot** the system – and type 'TMAKER' so that the screen looks as shown below:

A > TMAKER

You will then, after you have pressed the RETURN key, have a blank screen with a copyright notice at the top. If by any chance this does not happen then you must consult the T/Maker manual for instructions on how to customise the program for your computer. The 'WHAT NEXT?' prompt at the bottom of the screen is T/Maker's way of asking you what you want to choose from the commands available. There are a considerable number of these, but for our purposes we shall start with some which are relevant to word processing. These are words such as **create, data, align** and **edit**.

To create a new document you must tell T/Maker what the document is to be called and where it is to be stored. To do this you type:

DATA B CREATE MYTEXT EDIT

in response to the prompt, and you will be presented with a totally blank screen with the cursor flashing at the top left-hand corner. The command has told T/Maker that the document you are creating is to be stored on drive B, usually the right-hand drive, under the name of 'MYTEXT' when the 'save' command is issued. The 'edit' command sets T/Maker into the editing mode and you will see your commands flash along the bottom of the screen and you will be finally placed in the 'edit' mode and presented with a blank screen.

Most word processors provide you with a **ruler line** of some sort which tells you some useful information about the state of your document. T/Maker allows you a ruler line and it is called for by ESC ?. This means, like all the ESC sequences in the package, that you press ESC (the ESCAPE key) and then the ? key. It will tell you the number of lines your document consists of, how many characters it contains and the present position of the cursor. Thus 66/10 means that the cursor is in column 10 of line 66. If you do this before typing in your text you will have a screen which looks as shown in Figure 5.1. The mode code at the end is initially mode

Fig 5.1 *screen display on T/maker*

```
NAME: TMAKER.TXT  LINES: 25  FREE: 25735  LINE: 1/1  MODE: M
........1.........2.........3.........4.........5.........6.........7.........
1234567890123456789012345678901234567890123456789012345678901234567890123456789
```

M – the so-called 'manual' mode. This is a mode in which you have to start each new line by pressing the RETURN key, as with a typewriter. To get into the mode which allows you automatic wrap around of the text you need to press ESC R and you are then placed in 'drafting' mode, indicated by MODE: D at the end of the top line.

If you want to define the edges of your 'paper' you use what are called **wedges**. These do the same job as the margin stops in Wordcraft 80 and look quite similar. If you want text justified down the right-hand side of the paper you place a pair of > characters at the right hand end of the line and three < characters at the left-hand end of the line. Such a ruler line with margin stops is shown below:

```
<<<                                                      >>
```

So that everything typed after this ruler line has been typed in is set between these margins. This means that you have complete control over the way that your text looks on paper.

The ruler line controls the text until it is overruled by another ruler with different margin stops. This means that you can embed ruler lines in your text, without them being printed out, in cases where you need to have variable formats within your document. More uses for the ruler lines and their wedges will be described later on.

Now type a piece of text into your document. Remember that you have stated that it will be saved on drive B: under the name of 'mytext' when the time comes. Hence the name at the top of the ruler line when you go through the ESC ? sequence. Notice that as you type in your text the ruler line disappears from the top of the screen. ESC ? will cause it to be reinstated. Set up left-hand and right-hand margins at the 5th and 50th columns respectively and type in the text as shown below:

<<<   >>

T/Maker is a comprehensive computer package which combines word processing, spreadsheet calculations, list processing and file management. Once you have created a new blank file and set the word processor into 'edit' and put it into 'drafting' mode, by pressing ESC R, you are ready to to enter your text. Don't forget that because you are in 'drafting' mode you do not have to press the RETURN key unless you want to start a new paragraph.

Now at this point you might fall into the trap of thinking that the wedges have not worked as there is no justification in evidence. This is because the instruction to align the text has not yet been given and the screen will look as shown in Figure 5.2. First of all the cursor has to be moved to the

Fig 5.2 *text typed in*

```
        <<<                                    >>>
T/Maker is a comprehensive computer package which combines
word-processing, spreadsheet calculation, list processing
and file management. Once you have created a new blank file
and set the word-processor into "edit" and put it into "drafting"
mode, by pressing ESC R, you are ready to enter your text.
Don't forget that because you are in "drafting" mode you do
not have to press the RETURN key unless you want to start
a new paragraph.
```

beginning of the text and this is done by pressing ESC A. Then press CONTROL and Q simultaneously and you will find that you are returned to the WHAT NEXT? prompt. Your answer in this case is 'align'. The screen will blank out and after a few seconds will reappear as shown in Figure 5.3 with the text all nicely aligned under the margin stops. The WHAT NEXT? prompt reappears, to which you reply with 'edit' if you want to return to add more text or amend the existing text on the screen.

Combinations of CONTROL (sometimes ESC as well) and letter keys are used to move the cursor about the screen. A list of these follows:

CURSOR MOVES	COMMAND
Up one character	CONTROL – K
Down one character	CONTROL – J

Left one character	CONTROL - H
Right one character	CONTROL - L
Up one 'screenful'	ESC - CONTROL - K
Down one 'screenful'	ESC - CONTROL - J
Pan screen left	ESC - CONTROL - H
Pan screen right	ESC - CONTROL - L
Top left of screen	CONTROL - O
Top left of document	ESC - CONTROL - O
First line of document	ESC - A
Bottom line of document	ESC - Z
Move on one word	CONTROL - P
Move to end of line	ESC - CONTROL - P

Fig 5.3   *text after alignment*

```
<<<                              >>
T Maker is a comprehensive computer package
which combines word-processing, spreadsheet
calculation,   list   processing   and   file
management.   Once  you  have  created  a new
blank file and set  the  word-processor  into
"edit"  and  put it into "drafting" mode,  by
pressing ESC R,  you are ready to enter  your
text.   Don't  forget that because you are in
"drafting" mode you do not have to press  the
RETURN  key  unless  you  want to start a new
paragraph.
```

In order to amend the text at the cursor position there are a further set of commands. These are in the following list:

EFFECT	COMMAND
Delete character	CONTROL - E
Delete line	CONTROL - T
Delete all blanks before next character	CONTROL - U
Delet rest of line	CONTROL - Y
Insert mode	ESC - I
Insert blank line	CONTROL - R
Insert one space	CONTROL - W
Join with next line	ESC - <
Break into two lines	ESC - >

T/Maker allows you to 'overtype' so that a misspelt word can be corrected as you would on a typewriter – if the words are the same length! If you use the ESC - I command to insert text you must switch it off once you have inserted the additional text by another ESC – I after you have completed the insertion. Try using the insertion mode command to insert the following text into the paragraph you have already typed in:

> You can alter and amend text you have already entered by a series of simple keystrokes. You can move about the text by single characters, complete words or whole 'screenfuls' of text.

so that the text displayed on the screen looks as shown in Figure 5.4.

Fig 5.4 *screen display with new text inserted*

```
<<<                                          >>
T/Maker is a comprehensive  computer  package
which  combines word-processing,  spreadsheet
calculation,  list  processing  and  file
management.  Once  you  have  created  a new
blank  file and set  the  word-processor  into
"edit"  and  put  it  into  "drafting"  mode,  by
pressing ESC R,  you  are ready to enter  your
text.   You can alter and amend text you have
already  entered  by  a  series  of  simple
keystrokes.   You  can move about the text by
single  characters,  complete words  or  whole
"screenfuls"  of  text.   Don't  forget  that
because you are in "drafting" mode you do not
have  to press the RETURN key unless you  want
to start a new paragraph.
```

A word of warning about carrying out the above procedure. Since the text you are going to type in is quite long you will find that you do not get an automatic carriage return when the text falls outside the right-hand wedge. In fact, you will see that it disappears off the right-hand edge of the screen and you will be typing 'blind'. The best thing to do at this stage is to press RETURN and bring the cursor back to the screen. Then you can continue typing and see everything you type. This is like neither Wordstar nor Wordcraft as the cursor position is not of importance to the text except that it places characters at particular places on the screen. The alignment function does the 'cleaning up' and justification of the text: more of that in the next section.

5.2 CONTROLLING THE TEXT

First of all we need to show how text can be laid out on a page by the use of T/Maker's wedges. There are six variations.

The one which is being used at present for entering these lines of text is:

<<   >>

which ensures that the first word of the paragraph is indented if required and the right-hand edge of the text is justified so that we get a straight margin on both the left-hand and right-hand sides of the paper.

If, however, we use these wedges:

<<   ->>

the text still allows indentation at the start of the paragraph but provides a ragged right-hand margin; that is what the – sign in front of the right-hand wedges means, thus giving the impression that the text was typed on a conventional typewriter. If we use the following set of wedges the indentation is switched off and wherever the text starts on the line it will always be justified on the left-hand margins, but the right-hand margin will still be ragged.

<<<   ->>

The aligning command has been given precise instructions on how the text is to be laid out.

If we use the same wedges without the – sign at the right-hand edge then both edges are justified, like this:

<<<   >>

Our text is now held between the left-hand and right-hand margins and extra spaces are inserted between words in order to make every line the same length. T/Maker always places two spaces after each full stop.

<<–   >>

The above wedges centre the text.

The text is centred between the wedges and this allows us to produce headings.

The set of wedges below:

<<   ->>

allows us to indent and number paragraphs, so that we can have the following:

1. This is the first paragraph of a set of paragraphs.
2. This is the second paragraph. All we have to do is to type the paragraph number outside the left-hand pair of wedges and then start the text anywhere inside the wedges and the paragraph is automatically laid out for you.

If we altered the wedges to be:

<<   >>

we would get the same effect except that the right-hand edge will be justified and the ragged margin would disappear.

There are occasions when the alignment feature is not wanted – a good
example is when one is setting out a table in the text. This calls for an
instruction in the text to ignore the alignment feature. This is done by
displaying these wedges

>><<

so that the table shown below does not get distorted.

Country	Rate of Exchange per pound
France	11.90 francs
Germany	3.95 marks
Holland	4.43 guilders
U.S.A.	1.48 dollars

If we had not indicated that alignment was not required for this portion
of text the result would have been this:

Country Rate of Exchange per pound

France 11.90 francs Germany 3.95 marks Holland 4.43 guilders
U.S.A. 1.48 dollars

Don't worry if your document becomes littered with wedges all over the
place. They, like a number of other formatting instructions to T/Maker,
are embedded in the text and do not form part of the final printed document.

Between the margin wedges we can provide a number of tab stops. The
easiest way these can be inserted is to make sure that there are no tabs set
at all by pressing ESC – C – TAB, in that order. Then type a series of
characters, numbers would do, along a line in the positions where you
want the tabs to be. Then while the cursor is still on that line, press ESC –
S – TAB which says 'set tabs at the character positions on this line'. Then
the line can be deleted and the tab stops used. This is shown below. First
the tabs are cleared: ESC – C – TAB, then type:

and follow this by ESC – S – TAB while the cursor is on that line; and the
tabs are set up.

We can then use these tab stops to set up a table such as:

Mary	22	Single	London
Joan	25	Divorced	Birmingham
Tracey	30	Widow	Newquay
Helen	21	Single	Durham

As with other word processors, T/Maker allows for text to be moved about from one place to another or copied from one place to another. It does this by providing a special area of memory called a **buffer** into which lines of text can be 'dumped'. The CONTROL - G command places the current line of text into the buffer. This means that you place the cursor at the start of the line and press CONTROL - G. The line disappears. In fact, it has been copied into the buffer. If you move the cursor to another line and press CONTROL - G again that line, too, goes into the buffer. This is done for as many lines as you wish to have collected together in the buffer. Once you have selected the place for the contents of the buffer to be moved to you press CONTROL - D, and the whole contents of the buffer are written, starting at the place specified by the cursor position. If we use CONTROL - F instead of CONTROL - G the text is copied line by line into the buffer. CONTROL - D again will copy the contents of the buffer out to any specified place within the text. Figure 5.5 shows a piece of text and Figure 5.6 shows this text with part of it moved using CONTROL -Gs followed by CONTROL - D.

Fig 5.5 *piece of text before alteration using the buffer*

```
Here we have a piece of text which is going to have a section
moved from one place to another:=

Microcomputers are now becoming as common in offices as typewriters
and dictation machines. These machines place hitherto undreamed of
power of information storage and manipulation on the manager's
desk.

The new world of RAMs,floppy disks,word-processors and VDUs
can seem very confusing. This three-day course provides an
open door to the new technology.

The course will place emphasis on "hands-on" use of computers
and useful "packages", such as "T/Maker".
```

A useful job for this copying facility to do is that of, say, reproducing a standard heading for a table which is needed a number of times within the same document. All that is needed is to type the line once and then place it in the buffer. Then the buffer contents can be 'emptied' whenever required.

Fig 5.6 *text after alteration using the buffer*

```
ere we have a piece of text which is going to have a section
moved from one place to another:=
```

```
The new world of RAMs,floppy disks,word-processors and VDUs
can seem very confusing. This three-day course provides an
open door to the new technology.
```

```
Microcomputers are now becoming as common in offices as typewriters
and dictation machines. These machines place hitherto undreamed of
power of information storage and manipulation on the manager's
desk.
```

```
The course will place emphasis on "hands-on" use of computers
and useful "packages", such as "T/Maker".
```

If we want to clear the buffer in order to make way for more text to be moved about then CONTROL – C will do that. Note one thing, however: *lines copied into the buffer will be delivered out in the order in which they were read into the buffer.*

Very often when we are assembling tables in a document we want to juggle the columns about in order to even up the spaces between them. This can be very easily done with T/Maker using what they call a 'keystroke macro'.

Let us take the table we have already used:

Country	Rate of Exchange per pound
France	11.90 francs
Germany	3.95 marks
Holland	4.43 guilders
U.S.A.	1.48 dollars

and we want to move the right-hand column closer to the left-hand column. Perhaps we might want to move it four spaces to the left. First of all we place the cursor just before the topmost entry, the title in this case, of the column we want to move. Normally we would simply press the 'delete character' command keys (CONTROL – E) four times and then move down to the next line of the table and repeat the four keystrokes. So to move the title and four entries in the table we need twenty key strokes. If we place the cursor somewhere in the space between the two titles and press CONTROL – B we are placing the commands which follow into macro memory. Then we press CONTROL – E four times (four delete commands) and terminate with the macro-terminator which is – X. What this has done is store the commands so that a single keystroke will recall and execute them. Then all we have to do is to place the cursor successively between the columns and press CONTROL - X. This executes the macro-command 'delete four spaces' every time. So the table ends up as shown below:

Country	Rate of Exchange per pound
France	11.90 francs
Germany	3.95 marks
Holland	4.43 guilders
U.S.A.	1.48 dollars

Macro commands can be repeated, but this can cause difficulties sometimes, when placing the cursor in the position where the amendment is to take place and pressing CONTROL - Z. This causes the 'HOW MANY TIMES?' prompt to be displayed. All that is needed then is the number of times you want the macro to be executed to be keyed in and the rest happens automatically.

Finally in this section we will look at how T/Maker finds specified characters, or strings of characters, and replaces them if necessary. To set a search in motion we use the command ESC - '. This produces the prompt 'FIND WHAT STRING?' – as shown in Figure 5.7. If then we type in the

Fig 5.7 *setting a search in motion*

Now is the time for all good men to come to the aid of the party. The quick brown fox jumps over the lazy dog.

1/1 FIND WHAT STRING? quick

string to be found it will be highlighted by the cursor at its first appearance – as in Figure 5.8. If the next occurrence of the string is required then ESC - & will search again. ESC - & can be repeated for as long as the string is being sought after.

Fig 5.8 *the string highlighted*

```
Now is the time for all good men to come to the
aid of the party. The  uick brown fox jumps over
the lazy dog.
```

To find a string and then replace it with another string we use ESC - "
and we get the 'REPLACE WHAT STRING?' prompt. If we reply with the
string to be searched for followed by its replacement – as shown in Figure
5.9 – then as soon as the RETURN key is pressed the exchange is made.

Fig 5.9(a) *string to be replaced*

```
The quick brown fox jumps over the lazy dog. Now is the
time for all good men to come to the aid of the party.
```

```
1/1  REPLACE WHAT STRING?  the
```

Fig 5.9(b) *replacement string*

```
The quick brown fox jumps over the lazy dog. Now is the
time for all good men to come to the aid of the party.
```

```
1/1  WITH WHAT STRING?  a
```

The exchange, by the way, is made at every occurrence of the searched-for string, so be careful how this is used.

5.3 T/MAKER COMMANDS

You may remember from the first section on this word processor that the general T/Maker prompt at the bottom of the screen, 'WHAT NEXT?' is, in fact, asking just that. It is asking you to choose from the large number of commands which you can issue in response to that prompt, of which the commonest used in word processing are:

1. Data
2. Create
3. Get
4. Edit
5. Align
6. Save
7. Print
8. Files
9. Stop

T/Maker allows you to string a list of commands together and have them executed in the order you typed them in. For example, if you wanted to ensure that all data files, and that includes documents, are stored on drive B you would type:

DATA B

Then if you wanted to create a new file called 'TEXT1' you would type:

CREATE TEXT1

since after each command has been executed the prompt 'WHAT NEXT?' reappears. Having created a new file name you want to type text into it and this is done in 'edit' mode, so you type:

EDIT

However, to save time you can type:

DATA B CREATE TEXT1 EDIT

as shown in Figure 5.10, and you are straight away taken into the position where you can type text into the newly created blank document, hence the blank screen with the cursor blinking in the top left-hand corner.

When you are commencing entry of text into a new document you will almost certainly need to set up your margins, using the wedges and some tab stops. Then you type in your text and as you do so, having already

Fig 5.10   *creating a new file*

```
T/MAKER Version 3.02
Copyright (c) 1982
Peter Roizen
```

```
1/1  WHAT NEXT? DATA B CREATE TEXT1 EDIT
```

made sure that ESC - R has put you into 'drafting' mode, it appears ragged on the screen. You may well have to make additions and deletions even before you have reached the end of the text. This section of the book was written using T/Maker and it was found that it was very easy to travel around the document using the cursor keys to insert and delete sections of the text as required. There soon comes a point when you need to clean the text up since it is not automatically justified as with Wordcraft. It is very much like Wordstar in the sense that having amended the text you have to go back to a point before the amendments started and 'reformat'. However, with Wordstar you only reformat the paragraph on which the cursor lies. You reformat that part of the paragraph which comes after the cursor. With T/Maker, however, you reformat the whole of the text which comes after the cursor. Once you have moved the cursor to the point where you want the reformatting to commence you have to leave the 'edit' mode by pressing CONTROL - Q. At this point the 'WHAT NEXT?' prompt appears and you reply with

ALIGN

Having completed the alignment of the text, the screen blanks out and you are presented with 'cleaned-up' text when it reappears. The 'WHAT NEXT?' prompt is displayed at the bottom of the screen, as you are still in the 'command' mode, so to get back to the editing of your text you type

> EDIT

Of course, you may have completed your document at this point and may want to save it away on the disk you have previously specified (remember 'data b') So all you do is type:

> SAVE

and your file will be saved on the specified disk under the name you gave it when you created the file in the first place. The name is, in fact, first given to the 'working file' which is held in memory and whose length is given by the number following the word FREE on the line you get when you give the ESC - ? command. Typically this is around 20 000 bytes, i.e. 20 000 characters, but its size depends on the memory size of the computer you are using.

Alternatively, you may have completed your document and be ready to print it. If that is the case, you issue the printing instruction in response to the 'WHAT NEXT?' prompt. The print instruction is very flexible and easy to use. For example you could just type:

> PRINT IT

and this is sufficient to instruct T/Maker to commence printing the document currently held in memory. However, in order to give you a chance to see just what your document will look like when printed you can ask for the text to be 'printed' on the screen. After you have asked for printing to take place you will get a further prompt which says: 'NEXT PAGE 1 (YES.SCREEN.NO.GO.QUIT)?'

If you want to print reply with G. When the first complete page has been printed the prompt reappears, but this time with the page number changed to 2, as shown in Figure 5.11. A response of S prints page 2 on

Fig 5.11 *printing prompts*

NEXT PAGE 1 (YES.SCREEN.NO.GO.QUIT)? G

NEXT PAGE 2 (YES.SCREEN.NO.GO.QUIT)? Y

to the screen. If you reply with N page 2 is not printed and you are asked if you want page 3 to be printed. Q means that you want to leave the printing routine and return to 'WHAT NEXT?' If you reply to the 'NEXT PAGE?' query with G, for go, you will find that the current page and all the subsequent pages are printed out by the printer. As T/Maker proceeds with the printing of a many-paged document you will see a screen display as shown in Figure 5.12.

Fig 5.12 *screen display when printing a many-paged document*

NEXT PAGE 1   (YES.SCREEN.NO.GO.QUIT)? G

NEXT PAGE 2   (YES.SCREEN.NO.GO.QUIT)? Y

NEXT PAGE 3   (YES.SCREEN.NO.GO.QUIT)? Y

NEXT PAGE 4   (YES.SCREEN.NO.GO.QUIT)? Y

Note one thing, however, before you start printing. If you type:

    PRINT IT

make sure that the cursor has been moved to the start of the document. If you do not do that then printing starts at the current cursor position.

Another way of initiating printing is to type:

    GET MYTEXT PRINT IT

which will cause the document called 'mytext' to be loaded into memory. The cursor is automatically placed at the start of the text and then the 'NEXT PAGE...' prompt will appear. This will ensure that printing will start from the head of the document. Or you could simply type:

    PRINT MYTEXT

It is always possible that you may need to stop printing before the end of the document is reached. You may have found that you are printing the wrong document altogether or that you have spotted some error in the text as it is being printed. In order to terminate the printing you press CONTROL - Q.

A very useful thing to be able to do is to keep track of what we have stored on our disks. They have a very annoying habit of getting cluttered up with all sorts of files which we tend to forget about. In order to find out what files we have we can type:

    FILES

and after T/Maker has asked us for the drive, A or B, to be interrogated we will get a display as shown in Figure 5.13. Note that there are a number of files with the extention .BAK. These are back-up files which T/Maker sets

Fig 5.13 *display of file names*

PERFECT..MSS	CHAP3....BAK	FIG5.....BAK	FIG6.....BAK
CHAP4....BAK	NAMEFILE.BAK	CHAP1....BAK	LETTER...BAK
ADDRFILE.BAK	PARA1....BAK	CHAP2....BAK	DEMOFILE.BAK
FIG4.....BAK	CHAP5....	FIG9.....	FIG5.....
FIG7.....	FIG16....	FIG8.....	ADDRFILE.
FIG17....	CHAP3....	FIG6.....	FIG18....
LETTER1..	FIG20....	FIG19....	SORTFILE.
FIG21....	FIG23....	DATAFILE.	LFILE....
CHAP1....	DEMOFILE.	PRINTER..	ADDRESS..
PARA2....	PARA1....	FINISH...	LETTER2..
LETTER...	NUMBERS..	MYTEXT...	MYTEXT1..
CHAP2....	CHAP4....	FIG4.....	

up for us automatically and they are the files previous to the one last saved. In other words, a document called CHAP1 is created and text is typed into it then the document is saved. Subsequently we 'get' the file and add some more text to it, then we save this new version. What happens then is that the first version is not discarded, but saved under the title CHAP1.BAK and the latest version is now known as CHAP1. If the new version is then edited further then CHAP1.BAK is saved as the last version to be edited. This means that we can always go back to the earlier version we had before editing began. Wordstar provides, by the way, a similar facility.

If we want to get rid of any files we can type, say:

DELETE MYTEXT

and it is deleted from the disk.

Finally, in order to leave T/Maker having completed an editing session all we need to do is to type:

STOP

and we are returned to CP/M.

5.4 CONTROLLING THE OUTPUT

T/Maker provides a comprehensive series of instructions to control the look of the printed output apart from the wedges. It is possible, for example, to underscore text, to print it in bold face and to specify 'blocks' of text to be placed in special positions on the page.

First of all the underscoring: a complete line can be underscored by placing the code ' .‗' on the line immediately after the line to be under-scored. The code '.+' placed on the line after the text to be emboldened will provide the instruction to print the previous line in bold face type.

The two can be combined as shown in Figure 5.14 to make the line both underscored and emboldened.

Fig 5.14 *underscoring and emboldening text*

This is the line in question
.+
·_

Selected parts of a line may be underscored or emboldened by embedding instructions in the text. The '!' character placed before and after words will cause the 'bracketed' words to be emboldened and ' \ ' before and after words will cause them to be underlined. So with the commands shown in Figure 5.15(a) we get the results shown in Figure 5.15(b)

Fig 5.15(a) *commands for emboldening and underlining*

!FIRST!   \SECOND\   !\THIRD\!

FIRST   SECOND   THIRD

T/Maker allows us to put footnotes at the bottom of pages automatically. A footnote block is prefixed by the instruction '.footnote' and terminated by '.end', so that if I wanted to have a footnote at the bottom of this page I would type the block in now in the knowledge that it would be printed at the end of the current page, or at the end of the next page if there is not enough room for it at the end of the current page.

Blocks of text can be printed, for example, at the top and bottom of every page by the '.top', '.bottom' and '.end' instructions which in general are placed at the beginning of the document. With books it is common for the name of the book or the name of the chapter to be repeated at the head of every page. The number of the page is usually placed at the bottom of the page. The production of the manuscript for this section of the book was controlled by the instructions set out as shown in Figure 5.16. Notice that the '.top' instruction is followed by the words 'Mastering T/Maker' and this is followed by two blank lines and terminated by the instruction '.end'. The '.bottom' instruction is also three lines long with a '#' sign in the middle of the second line. This will cause the page number to be printed in that position. You can put whatever text you wish inside the top and bottom routines and they will always be printed at the head and foot of each page.

We can define the size of the printed page for T/Maker by using the

Fig 5.16 *page layout instructions*

```
.top
Mastering T/Maker


.end
.bottom


                              ✦


.end
```

'.pagesize', '.length', '.width' and '.new' instructions. The first three of these are placed at the head of the document. The first one defines the length of the printed page, which for standard printer paper is 66, that is, 66 lines of printing available per page. The length of the text is the number of actual lines of print we want on each page. The width instruction tells the printer the maximum number of columns to print: this is usually 80. So the beginning of the document which constitutes this section of our manuscript looked as shown in Figure 5.17.

Fig 5.17 *layout instructions for text*

```
.top
Mastering T/Maker


.end
.bottom


                              ✦


.end
.width 80
.pagesize 66
.length 62
```

Another very useful feature gained by the use of blocks of text is being able to 'bind' together certain sections to ensure that they do not get printed across two pages. This is particularly useful if one has a table which would look bad if it was a short table with the first half printed at the bottom of one page and the second half at the top of the next page.

We can deal with this by marking the start of the table with '.block' and the end with '.end', as shown in Figure 5.18.

Fig 5.18 *'binding together' sections of text*

```
.block
This is a table which must all be printed on one page

        Computer      Price      RAM        Disc Capacity
.+

.-


        Sirius        2395       128K       1200K
        IBM           2884       128K       640K
        Future        1850       128K       1600K
        Olivetti      2900       128K       320K

.end
```

We can use a number of the T/Maker facilities to produce personalised letters or address labels. For example, if we create a table of names, addresses and the appropriate salutations we can create a series of personalised letters quite easily. The table is kept on a file called, in this case, 'addrfile'. It is shown below:

Name	Addr1	Addr2	Postcode	Salutation
+ Miss S. Hay	22 Cheyne Walk	Chelmsford	CH2 3ER	Dear Sally
+ Sir J. French	'Court Lodge'	Walmer Kent	DE3 6TY	Dear Sir John
+ Mr G. Jones	14 Kings Walk	Stamford	PE9 2QS	Dear Mr Jones
+ Mr F. Taylor	34 Elm Road	Warton Salop	SA7 5RG	Dear Fred

We are going to send a letter to each of the people in the address file so that it has their name and address printed in the correct place and the appropriate salutation printed before the body of the letter. The first thing that has to be done is to produce what is called a 'mask' which converts the table into a column of records. The mask defines the start and finish of each field in the address file by means of curly braces, {and } . The mask looks like this:

```
+ {1          }{          }{          }{          }{          }
+ {           }{          }{          }{          }{          }
+ {           }{          }{          }{          }{          }
+ {           }{          }{          }{          }{          }
```

This mask is saved on disk under the name of 'DATAFILE' and then 'ADDRFILE' is loaded into memory. The mask is then 'unloaded' into 'DATAFILE' by the command:

UNLOAD DATAFILE

and the screen shows the following:

```
 1 = 'Mr. G. Jones'
 2 = '14 Kings Walk'
 3 = ' Stamford'
 4 = 'PE9 2QS'
 5 = 'Dear Mr Jones'
 6 = 'Miss S. Hay'
 7 = '22 Cheyne Walk'
 8 = 'Chelmsford'
 9 = 'CH2 3ER'
10 = 'Dear Sally'
11 = 'Sir J. French'
12 = ' "Court Lodge" '
13 = 'Walmer KENT'
14 = 'DE3 6TY'
15 = 'Dear Sir John'
16 = 'Mr F. Taylor'
17 = '34 Elm Road'
18 = 'WARTON Salop'
19 = 'SA7 5RG'
20 = 'Dear Fred'
```

This is now a file of 20 'fields' and it is then saved under the name of IFILE'. Next a letter is written which contains the curly braces, { and } , to show where the records from the newly created 'IFILE' are to be filled in. Using the copy instructions copies of the letter are made in a single file, one copy for each customer. A typical letter blank looks like that shown in Figure 5.19.

The letter file is then loaded into memory and the command:-

LOAD IFILE

is given and the letters have the appropriate names, addresses and salutations loaded in at the appropriate places. There must be one blank letter in the file for each client. A '.new' instruction must be placed at the end of each letter. This ensures that each one is printed on a new page.

We can organise the printing of our letters by using T/Maker's extended command strings, like this:

GET LETTER LOAD IFILE PRINT IT

The resulting letters are shown in Figure 5.20.

T/Maker, in fact, offers us a number of other facilities which we can

Fig 5.19 *typical letter blank*

```
                              U.T.C.Trading Co,Ltd.,
                              U.T.C.House,
                              Warton,
                              Norfolk,
                              NR3 6DX
```

1st January 1984

```
(1            )
(             )
(             )
(        )


(              )
```

I am pleased to inform you that our new range of floppy discs
and accessories are now available. The latest price list is
enclosed. As valued and regular customers we are pleased to

offer you special discounts on all purchases made before the
end of the current month.

Assuring you of our best attention at all times.

Yours sincerely,

J.Barton
Sales Manager

.new

Fig 5.20 *letters printed out*

U.T.C.Trading Co,Ltd.,
U.T.C.House,
Wharton,
Norfolk,
NR4 6QR

1st January 1984

Miss S.Hay
22 Cheyne Walk
Chelmsford
CH2 3ER

Dear Sally

I am pleased to inform you that our new range of floppy discs
and accessories are now available. The latest price list is
enclosed. As valued and regular customers we are pleased to
offer you special discounts on all purchases made before the
end of the current month.

Assuring you of our best attention at all times.

Yours sincerely,

J.Barton
Sales Manager

Fig 5.20 *continued*

U.T.C.Trading Co,Ltd.,
U.T.C.House,
Warton,
Norfolk,
NR3 6DX

1st January 1984

Sir J.French
"Court Lodge"
Walmer KENT
DE3 6TY

Dear Sir John

I am pleased to inform you that our new range of floppy discs
and accessories are now available. The latest price list is
enclosed. As valued and regular customers we are pleased to
offer you special discounts on all purchases made before the
end of the current month.

Assuring you of our best attention at all times.

Yours sincerely,

J.Barton
Sales Manager

Fig 5.20 *continued*

```
                              U.T.C.Trading Co,Ltd.,
                              U.T.C.House,
                              Warton,
                              Norfolk,
                              NR3 6DX
```

1st January 1984

Mr.G.Jones
14 Kings Walk
Stamford
PE9 2QS

Dear Mr Jones

I am pleased to inform you that our new range of floppy discs
and accessories are now available. The latest price list is
enclosed. As valued and regular customers we are pleased to
offer you special discounts on all purchases made before the
end of the current month.

Assuring you of our best attention at all times.

Yours sincerely,

J.Barton
Sales Manager

Fig 5.20 *continued*

U.T.C.Trading Co,Ltd.,
U.T.C.House,
Warton,
Norfolk,
NR3 6DX

1st January 1984

Mr.F.Taylor
34 Elm Road
WARTON Salop
SA7 5RG

Dear Fred

I am pleased to inform you that our new range of floppy discs
and accessories are now available. The latest price list is
enclosed. As valued and regular customers we are pleased to
offer you special discounts on all purchases made before the
end of the current month.

Assuring you of our best attention at all times.

Yours sincerely,

J.Barton
Sales Manager

put to work on the files it keeps. For example, our ‚ADDRFILE' can be sorted by a simple instruction so that the names of the towns will be placed in alphabetical order. The instruction given would be:

GET ADDRFILE SORT S 33 39

This tells T/Maker that the file called 'ADDRFILE' is to be sorted on the field in columns 33 to 39 (the first seven characters of the town names). The S instructions that only those entries with a + sign in front are to be sorted – otherwise the contents of the title will be sorted as well! The result is:

Name	Addr1	Addr2	Postcode	Salutation
+ Miss S. Hay	22 Cheyne Walk	Chelmsford	CH2 3ER	Dear Sally
+ Mr G. Jones	14 Kings Walk	Stamford	PE9 2QS	Dear Mr Jones
+ Mr F. Taylor	34 Elm Road	Warton Salop	SA7 5RG	Dear Fred
+ Sir J. French	'Court Lodge'	Walmer Kent	DE3 6TY	Dear Sir John

Finally, we can link together a number of pre-written files, in this case standard paragraphs for letters, into a final complete letter personalised for one client.

This involves the use of a command which contains the instruction '.continue filename'. By including this in the document we tell T/Maker to fetch and print that file at that point of the document. For the next example we have four files already written and saved on disk. They are called 'ADDRESS', 'PARA1', 'PARA2' and 'FINISH' and they look like this:-

'HEADING' is the file which contains the address of the company from whom the letter is sent:'

```
U.T.C.Trading Co.,Ltd.,
U.T.C.House,
Wharton,
Norfolk,
NR4 6QT
```

Then there is 'PARA1' which is:

```
Thank  you for you enquiry regarding opening an account
with us.  We shall require a banker's reference and two
references from traders with which you have had  credit
accounts for at least two years.
```

'PARA2' is the file which contains:

```
If your references are satisfactory we shall be pleased
to  allow  you a credit limit of £2,000 subject  to the
settlement  of  your account  within  the  month  of
peresentation of the statement.
```

and finally the closing paragraph is:

```
Assuring you of our best attention at all times.

Yours very sincerely,


H. L. Kindon
Credit Manager
```

The letter which binds these all together is shown in Figure 5.21.

When the command to print the above letter is given the output is shown in Figure 5.22.

Fig 5.21 *instructions 'binding' letter together*

```
                    continue address


            13th March 1984



            M.E.Sullivan Esq.,
            M.B.Electronics,
            Unit 43,
            Western Industrial Estate,
            Westchester,
            Cumbria.


            Dear Mr.Sullivan,

            .continue para1

            .continue para2


            .continue finish
```

Fig 5.22 *letter printed out*

```
                                        U.T.C.Trading Co.,Ltd.,
                                        U.T.C. House,
                                        Warton,
                                        Norfolk,
                                        NR3 6DX


13th March 1984



M.E.Sullivan Esq.,
M.B.Electronics,
Unit 43,
Western Industrial Estate,
Westchester,
Cumbria.


Dear Mr.Sullivan,


Thank you for your enquiry regarding  opening  an  account
with  us.   We  shall require a banker's reference and two
references from traders with which  you  have  had  credit
accounts for at least two years.


If your references are satisfactory we shall be pleased to
allow  you  a  credit  limit  of  £2,000  subject  to  the
settlement  of  your  account  within  the  month  of
presentation of the statement.


Assuring you of our best attention at all times.

Yours very sincerely,


H.L.Kindon
Credit Manager
```

T/Maker III provides very powerful word-processing facilities without having to recourse to complicated multi-key operations for most of the commands. The main system commands are given in English – CREATE, ALIGN, PRINT and so forth – and can be strung together in command lines. Blocks of text can easily be bound together for clarity – footnotes as an example. The exact look of the printed page can be previewed on the screen although page breaks are not displayed as the creation of text takes place. The creation of personalised letters is slightly complicated but very effective. Searching and replacement of text can only be made for characters without embedded blanks. In other words, only single words can be searched for, not phrases.

VIEW

6.1 INTRODUCING VIEW

View is one of the word-processing packages available for the BBC micro-computer. It differs in several respects from the other word processors described in this book because it is supplied as a chip which is plugged into a spare socket inside the case of the machine – see Figure 6.1. This means that as soon as the computer is switched on you have word processing available immediately. There are no programs to load and no keys to press in order to get it started. In addition, when you purchase View you are provided with an overlay strip which fits round the special orange-coloured function keys at the top of the keyboard. This shows that each of the ten function keys can control any one of three separate operations depending on whether the key is pressed on its own or in conjunction with either of the CONTROL or SHIFT keys. This is shown in Figure 6.2. As soon as the computer is switched on it will display the following on the screen:

```
View A1.4
No text
Editing no file
Screen Mode 7
Printer default
=>
```

This tells us the version of View we are using – A1.4 in this case – and the fact that there is no file in memory being edited. 'Screen Mode 7' provides you with a screen containing 24 lines of text with 34 charac-ters on each one of them. The 'printer default' message does not say that there is anything wrong but that the printer is available straight away for you to use. With most word processors you have to go through a process called 'configuring the printer'. This is because there are so

Fig 6.1 *View plugs into the case of the computer*

many different types of printer around that their different characteristics have to be given to the word-processor program before printing takes place. The BBC computer is no exception to this and the instructions on how to set up the computer to 'talk' to any particular printer are given in the BBC Microsystem User Guide and this should be consulted before connecting a printer. Once the computer is set up for your particular printer you can usually forget about it.

In case you should think that your screen with 24 lines of 34 characters is rather small you should remember that the screen is only acting as a 'window' on the complete text you are editing and you can have lines in your document of up to 132 characters long. You can move around the document with ease, viewing any part you wish by using the arrow keys which are placed at the top right-hand corner of the keyboard. If you press an arrow key and the SHIFT key simultaneously you can move horizontally one word at a time or vertically 24 lines at a time. If you want to see more of the text at one viewing then you can change the mode. For example Mode 0 supplies you with a screen of 31 lines with 76

Fig 6.2 *keyboard with View overlay strip*

characters on each and you change mode by typing Mode 0 but you must do this in the 'command' mode and not while you are entering text. More about 'command' and 'text' modes shortly. Be careful, however; each mode allows you different amounts of memory to store the text while it is being edited. Mode 7 allows you over 25 000 bytes (i.e. characters) and Mode 0 only allows you 5000.

There may be some confusion over the use of the word 'mode' in two different ways. As with Wordcraft we have several modes of operation, which are nothing to do with the screen modes. View in fact has two operating modes called 'command' mode and 'text' mode. These are similar to the 'command' and 'type modes of Wordcraft, 'text' mode is the mode in which you can enter text into a document and edit it. The other mode is that which allows you to print text and control its style of output in just the same way as with Wordcraft. One thing about the View word processor is that documents can be saved on tape using an ordinary domestic cassette player as well as on the faster but more expensive disks. This does mean that you can get used to the features of a word processor for a very small outlay compared with the others.

Having started up the computer you are automatically in 'command' mode and the computer is waiting for you to tell it what to do. First of all you need to press the CAPS LOCK key. This is because the keyboard is locked into capitals only at start-up time; this is shown by the central light of the three at the bottom left of the keyboard being illuminated. As your text will usually consist of both capitals and lower case text you will need to select these in the same way as you would with a typewriter, by using SHIFT. If you are going to start by typing in a new piece of text from scratch you first of all type the word NEW. The display on the screen then informs you how many bytes of memory are available to you. Remember that one byte represents one key depression. As with Wordcraft, when you reach the memory limit you need to save the text away. In fact, View informs you by 'bleeping' at you when you are about to reach the limit. You can always see how much memory you have left by going into 'command' mode. You select 'text' mode by pressing the ESCAPE key and to get back into 'command' mode you press it again.

Once you have selected 'text' mode you will see a series of dots and asterisks across the top of the screen. This is the 'ruler' line giving the layout of the page which you get by default – that is, without any prompting from you. Each dot or asterisk represents a character position and the < at the right-hand end of the ruler represents the right-hand margin. The stars represent built-in tab stops and you can move the cursor to any one of the tab positions by pressing the TAB key. For example, if the ruler is as follows:

        . . . . * . . . . * . . . . * . . . . * . . . . * . <

and you press the TAB key once you will print

                in this position

but if you press the TAB key twice you will print

                        in this position

and so on.

You can change the layout of the ruler to allow for the setting-out of documents in various ways. The length of the ruler depends on the mode in which you start up; the larger the number of characters allowed in memory by the mode, the longer the default ruler.

You can set up your own ruler lines in the text by typing in the ruler line you want, place the cursor anywhere on it and press the 'mark as ruler' keys, that is CONTROL and F8. Then you type in the series of dots and asterisks which will define your new ruler. On pressing RETURN the new ruler appears at the top of the screen and that is the one obeyed from then onward. The < and > characters specify the left and right margins. But we digress; we must get down to using the word processor for entering and modifying text before we enter into a long explanation of the more esoteric features of View.

Type in the following text; remembering that you do not have to press RETURN at the end of every line. View wraps words round from line to line and as it does so the paragraph will be automatically justified – that is what FJ at the top of the screen tells us. FJ means 'format and justify'.

> The View word-processing package for the BBC microcomputer system offers a cheap introduction to the technique of word processing. Documents can be stored on cassette tapes as well as disks, and the View program is stored completely in a plug-in ROM (Read Only Memory) chip. A self-adhesive strip fits over the ten programmable function keys at the top of the keyboard and will remind you of the operations you can perform on the text using those keys.

Inserting new text is very simple. All you have to do is to place the cursor – using the arrow keys – at the place in the text where you want to type in your extra characters and go into 'insert' mode. This you do by pressing CONTROL and F4. The letter I appears in the top left-hand corner of the screen. Then you can type in your extra text. When you have completed your typing you press the same pair of keys again. In order to test this procedure insert the following sentence after the first sentence of the text you have already typed in:

> You have to remove the cover of the microcomputer and plug the View chip in according to the instructions given to you by Acorn.

You will then have your text looking like this:

> The View word-processing package for the BBC microcomputer system offers a cheap introduction to the technique of word processing. You have to remove the cover of the microcomputer and plug the View chip in according to the instructions supplied by Acorn. Documents can be stored on cassette tapes as well as disks, and the View program is stored completely in a plug-in ROM (Read Only Memory) chip. A self-adhesive strip fits over the ten programmable function keys at the top of the keyboard and will remind you of the operations you can perform on the text using those keys.

Your amended paragraph will now have a ragged right-hand edge because of the text you have inserted. All that has to be done is to move the cursor to the beginning of the paragraph and press the 'format block' key – key F0. Your text will then be aligned with a straight right-hand margin.

6.2 EDITING WITH VIEW

First of all we need to be able to insert single characters into text we have already written. For this we use the 'insert character' key – F8. We simply place the cursor at the point where the extra character is to be inserted and press F8. A space opens up and we can type in our extra character. It is exactly the same as Wordcraft in this respect. So we can go from:

COLOR

to

COLO R

and

COLOUR

easily. Notice that the characters to the right of the insertion are all moved one space to the right.

To delete parts of the text you can:

1. Delete a single character by pressing the DELETE key at the bottom right of the keyboard to delete the character to the left of the cursor, or you can press F9 to delete the character at the cursor position.
2. Delete from the cursor position up to a specified character. You press SHIFT and F3 to 'delete up to character' followed by the character which terminates your deletion.
3. Delete the part of the line from the cursor position ot the end of the line – press F3 for 'delete end of line'.
4. Delete a complete line of text – press 'delete line' which is key F7.

To move quickly around the text without using the arrow keys we can go to the start of the document by using 'top of text' – key F1. We can go to the end of the document using 'bottom of text' – key F2. We can move the cursor to the beginning of the line by using key F4 and to the end of the line by using key F5.

At the top left of the screen there are the letters FJ. As mentioned earlier these indicate that the word processor is in 'format' and 'justify' mode. In 'format' mode any word which will not fit into the space left on the current line will be transferred to the beginning of the next line. 'Justify' mode has the effect of inserting extra spaces into each line so producing a straight right-hand margin. The two modes are controlled by the keys F2 and F3 pressed simultaneously with the CONTROL key as shown by the table at the top of the keyboard. Try entering text with both 'format' and 'justify' off and then with just one of them on. You have already seen how to reformat a piece of text using the 'format block' key. This only operates when you are in 'format' mode. If you are in 'justify' mode as well, as you are by default, then the text is justified. If not, and you are in 'format' mode alone, you will get formatted text, i.e. conforming to the margins, but with a ragged right-hand edge.

Another way of moving around a piece of text is to ask View to search for a particular word. In order to do this we go into 'command' mode, by pressing ESCAPE, then we type the word 'SEARCH' followed by the word to be search for and after the RETURN key has been pressed the searching takes place. If the word is found then the 'text' mode is selected and the cursor flashes at the required word. A useful feature of View is that if you are not quite certain how the word you are looking for is spelt you can use 'wild cards' in the word. For example, if you are looking for the word 'certain' which you think may have been spelt incorrectly, then you type:

SEARCH CER????

On pressing RETURN the first occurrence of the first letters, and in this case any other four letters following, will be found and the cursor will be placed at the word we are looking for. If we press 'next match' – CONTROL and F1 – then the next match will be found. This can be continued until the word we require is finally found.

If we want to change a word from another whenever it appears we can use, again from 'command' mode, the instruction 'CHANGE' and the change will take place throughout the document. This has to be used with care since you have no allowance for choosing whether or not you want the change to take place. For example, if you have the text:

Since we have had a Conservative government we have been able to carry out all the policies outlined in the Conservative manifesto. This shows that a Conservative government honours its pledges.

Then we go into 'command' mode and type:

CHANGE Conservative Labour

and after the RETURN key has been pressed we get the following:

Since we have had a Labour government we have been able to carry out all the policies outlined in the Labour manifesto. This shows that a Labour government honours its pledges.

'CHANGE' changes every occurrence of one string for another without asking. If we use 'REPLACE' we get the choice of replacement.

We can mark text by using up to six markers. We do this by pressing 'set marker' – SHIFT and F7 – at which point MK appears in the top left-hand corner of the screen. We then press 1 to identify the start and then move the cursor to the end and identify the end of the text with marker 2. Then we can:

1. Delete a marked block of text by pressing 'delete block' – CONTROL and F0.

2. Move a block of text by placing the cursor at the point where we want the text to be moved to and press 'move', which is SHIFT and F0.
3. Copy a block of text by doing the same as above except that we press the COPY key, which is in the bottom right-hand corner.

If we want to clear markers from the text we press the ESCAPE key.

If we want to centre text between margins we use the CE command set in the text to be centred. It is done like this: press the 'edit command key – SHIFT and F8 – and then type CE followed by RETURN. This sets the letters CE in the left-hand margin outside the text and causes the line in which the command is typed to be centred.

Other text-embedded commands are RJ for 'right-justify'. Again you press SHIFT and F8 and then RJ, RETURN and the text which follows is justified to the right-hand margin:

Like this
and like this.

Similarly, we can enter commands to set the page length – PL followed by RETURN and the number of lines to be printed on one page. We can amend the line spacing with LS, RETURN and the number of spaces between successive lines of the text in order to obtain single, double or triple spacing.

If we want to instruct the printer to start the next piece of printing on a new page we have to tell it to 'eject' the current page. This is done wih the PE command, which is inserted in the same way as the other text-embedded commands (SHIFT –FB followed by PE).

There are other similar commands referred to in the manual concerning the arrangement of margins at the top and bottom and on the left.

If you press 'edit' command followed by DH you define a heading which consists of three components: the part on the left of a page, the centre and on the right separated by / signs. In the manuscript of this book we had:

DH/Mastering View///

thus causing the words 'Mastering View' to be printed in the top left-hand corner of each page. Similarly we use the DF command to define the 'footer' for each page in a similar manner. As we usually need to print the page number in the centre of the page at the bottom we can put:

DF//IP//

where IP is the instruction to print the current page number in that position.

View allows us to print text underlined or in bold characters, achieved on a printer by what is called 'double strike'. In order to define the underlined text we press the HIGHLIGHT 1 key, SHIFT and F4 before the text to be underlined and again after we want the underlining to finish. Similarly, we can specify the start and the finish of bold type by pressing HIGHLIGHT 2, SHIFT and F5 before and after the text to be emboldened.

Text is saved and loaded from the 'command' mode and it is done very simply by pressing ESCAPE while in 'text' mode – this takes you into the 'command' mode – and typing

    SAVE"TEXTNAME"

and *don't forget the inverted commas* – View is very fussy about them. If you are in 'command' mode and wish to load a previously saved file you type:

    LOAD"TEXTNAME"

View also provides the facility of loading a previously saved file into an existing file, merging a document saved on disk with the one currently in memory. In addition we can save a marked piece of text from the current document on to disk. The commands for this are 'READ' and 'WRITE'.

6.3 PRINTING TEXT

View allows us to control the way our text looks on the printed page. The creation of headers, footers and page eject commands embedded in the text have already been dealt with, but there are others. For example, we can define margins at the top and bottom as well as on the left of each page. The page length and the line spacing are also controllable. All these commands are placed in the text by means of the 'edit command' key, SHIFT and F8. This always places the two characters typed in after the command in the left-hand margin of the text on the screen. These are:

    TM – Top margin (The number of lines above the header.)
    BM – Bottom margin (The number of lines below the footer.)
    HM – Header margin (The number of lines between header and text.)
    FM – Footer margin (The number of lines between text and footer.)
    PL – Page length
    LS – Line spacing

After the RETURN key has been pressed a number is entered giving the number of lines in each of the margins, the number of lines in each page or the spacing of the lines on the page. We could therefore have a set of embedded commands giving the layout of each page of our text as follows:

```
PL    40
LS    2
LM    5
DH//CATALOGUE//
DF//PAGE IP//
TM    1
BM    1
HM    1
FM    1
```

and our page would consist of one blank line at the top with the word 'CATALOGUE' in the centre of the next line followed by one blank line; then there would be one blank line below the text, the page number in the form 'PAGE XX' with another blank line at the bottom. The whole page would be 40 lines long with a margin of five spaces on the left.

Now comes the concept of the 'macro'. This is a piece of text which acts as a 'skeleton' into which pieces of text such as names and addresses together with other information can be placed. A macro is used for producing personalised letters for example. The macro is first of all defined and given a two-letter name. This is done by another embedded command obtained by pressing 'edit command' and typing DM for 'define Macro'. This places DM in the left-hand margin and we follow this by a two-letter identifier. So for a macro called 'LE' for 'LEtter' we would have:

DM LE

Then follows the body of the text into which various 'customising' features are inserted. So we might get this:

Union Electrical Co
43 Tower Street
Lullhampton
Devon PL19 5TH

21st March 1984

@0
@1
@2
@3
@4

@5

We have pleasure in enclosing our latest brochure of home video games and entertainment. I am sure that you will be the envy of all your neighbours in @3 when you are seen to be the proud winner of our free prize draw, details of which are enclosed. Only one prize is being allocated to your area and you, @0, could be the lucky winner.

Good luck and best wishes

Yours very sincerely

J. T. Welcome
Sales Manager
PE
EM
LE Mr J. Howard, 'The Walnuts', Lime Avenue, Luton, Beds, Dear Mr Howard
LE Mrs Eva Knott, The Sweet Shoppe, West Parade, Seeford, Hants, Dear Eva
LE Mr J. Dill, School House, Eye Road, Haveram, Norfolk, Dear Mr Dill

This document is then saved and when printed the file of names addresses and salutations stored at the bottom are inserted in turn into the text. '@0' stands for the first field of a line – the name in this case, @1 stands for the second and so on. The embedded LE is the name of the macro into which that set of information is to be inserted. This means that we get one letter sent to Mr Howard, one to Mrs Knott and so on. In other words there is one letter for each line of data.

You will notice that the text of the letter has deliberately been left 'ragged', by turning justification off. This is because if the text had been justified on entry each paragraph would not be reformatted on printing, as happens with other word processors. So we make the text look more as if it had been typed, otherwise one line would be longer than the others and make the insertion obvious. The printed letters are shown in Figure 6.3.

The following is another use of a macro. It is a piece of text – a wedding invitation in fact – with part of the guest list following, just as before. The lines prefixed with the CE commands allow the text to be centred when it is printed. The macro is known as 'IN' – for 'INvitation'. The whole document including the guest list is saved and then printed, thus producing a series of individually printed invitations.

Fig 6.3 *complete letter printed out*

* * *

Union Electrical Co
43 Tower Street
Lullhampton
Devon PL19 5TH

21st March 1984

Mrs Eva Knott
The Sweet Shoppe
West Parade
Seeford
Hants

Dear Eva

We have pleasure in enclosing our latest brochure of
home video games and entertainment. I am sure that you
will be the envy of all your neighbours in Seeford
when you are seen to be the proud winner of our free
prize draw, details of which are enclosed. Only one
prize is being allocated to your area and you, Mrs Eva
Knott, could be the lucky winner.

Good luck and best wishes

Yours very sincerely

J.T.Welcome
Sales Manager

Fig 6.3 continued

* * *

Union Electrical Co
43 Tower Street
Lullhampton
Devon PL19 5TH

21st March 1984

Mr J.Howard
The Walnuts
Lime Avenue
Luton
Beds

Dear Mr Howard

We have pleasure in enclosing our latest brochure of
home video games and entertainment. I am sure that you
will be the envy of all your neighbours in' Luton when
you are seen to be the proud winner of our free prize
draw, details of which are enclosed. Only one prize is
being allocated to your area and you, Mr J.Howard,
could be the lucky winner.

Good luck and best wishes

Yours very sincerely

J.T.Welcome
Sales Manager

* * *

Fig 6.3 continued

* * *

Union Electrical Co
43 Tower Street
Lullhampton
Devon PL19 5TH

21st March 1984

Mr J.Dill
School House
Eye Road
Haveram
Norfolk

Dear Mr Dill

We have pleasure in enclosing our latest brochure of
home video games and entertainment. I am sure that you
will be the envy of all your neighbours in Haveram
when you are seen to be the proud winner of our free
prize draw, details of which are enclosed. Only one
prize is being allocated to your area and you, Mr
J.Dill, could be the lucky winner.

Good luck and best wishes

Yours very sincerely

J.T.Welcome
Sales Manager

* * *

DM IN

White Heather
Hill Road
Warmington on Sea
Suffolk

CE	Mr & Mrs F. J. West
CE	Have pleasure in inviting
CE	@0
CE	To the wedding of their daughter
CE	Mary Louise
CE	to
CE	Mr Jeremy Cardhouse
CE	on Saturday November 5th 1983
CE	at 12.00 noon
CE	at St Marks Church
CE	Reception at home
RJ	R.S.V.P.
PE	
EM	
IN	Mr & Mrs S. Lyon
IN	Lord and Lady Mellors
IN	Mr Simon Smith

The printed invitations will look as shown in Figure 6.4.

You can get some idea of the way your text will appear on the printer by pressing ESCAPE to get into 'command' mode and then:

SCREEN filename

whereupon your document is 'printed' on the screen as it will appear when printed out. You are presented with a 'screenful' at a time and this is scrolled up when the SHIFT key is pressed. Remember, however, that when you print to the screen that you must make sure that you are in a mode which enables you to see a full page width of your text, otherwise you will get a 'wrap around' which makes it very difficult to see what is happening. Mode 3 is probably the best one to use.

View is a very easy word processor to use and despite the fact that there are no helpful menus available, there are the function keys which are very clearly marked. Once you know your way around these you can edit text very easily. There are certain things that View will not do, decimal tabbing being one of them. The choice of modes for the screen display is rather confusing at first since you have to equate the amount of memory

Fig 6.4 *wedding invitations printed out*

```
                              White Heather
                              Hill Road
                              Warmington on Sea
                              Suffolk


          Mr & Mrs F.J.West
       Have pleasure in inviting
          Mr & Mrs S.Lyon
     To the wedding of their daughter
             Mary Louise
                 to
          Mr Jeremy Cardhouse
     on Saturday November 5th 1983
            at 12.00 noon
          at St Marks Church
          Reception at home
                              R.S.V.P.

                              White Heather
                              Hill Road
                              Warmington on Sea
                              Suffolk


          Mr & Mrs F.J.West
       Have pleasure in inviting
          Lord and Lady Mellors
     To the wedding of their daughter
             Mary Louise
                 to
          Mr Jeremy Cardhouse
     on Saturday November 5th 1983
            at 12.00 noon
          at St Marks Church
          Reception at home
                              R.S.V.P.

                              White Heather
                              Hill Road
                              Warmington on Sea
                              Suffolk


          Mr & Mrs F.J.West
       Have pleasure in inviting
          Mr Simon Smith
     To the wedding of their daughter
             Mary Louise
                 to
          Mr Jeremy Cardhouse
     on Saturday November 5th 1983
            at 12.00 noon
          at St Marks Church
          Reception at home
                              R.S.V.P.
```

your document is likely to need with the need to see the full width of the text. However, you do get a warning 'bleep' when the memory is getting full. View certainly has a very full range of facilities which one can quickly become familiar with.

WORD PROCESSING
EXAMPLES

The examples shown on the following pages are typical of the type of work which can be performed using a word processor. They were all produced by the same word processor and should all be capable of being reproduced on any other, perhaps not looking quite the same, but with a basically similar layout. When you have access to a word processor try out the facilities offered after you have given the suggestions in the text a try. Example 2 shows a typical draft from a manual which has been edited by hand. What you should aim to do is to produce a clean, edited page using the handwritten amendments.

EXAMPLE 1

Micro Experts Ltd
23 High Street
Westchester
Hants
PO3 2QS

21st February 1984

Mr.J.C.Williams
Sorbo Tennis Balls Ltd
Industrial Estate
Newchester
Dorset
BO7 8RD

Dear Mr. Williams

Thank you very much for your enquiry. We should be pleased
to quote you for a computer system to handle your stock
control. Our representative, Mr.Brewer, will be pleased to
call on you at any time convenient to yourselves. In order
to arrange a suitable time he will be telephoning you
during the new few days.

We feel sure that we can satisfy your particular
requirements within the price range you have specified.

Yours sincerely

J.K.Burton
Sales Director

142

EXAMPLE 2

Centre + make bold

DTI FORMS TERMINAL

The design of traditional computer terminals has not been overly concerned with its part in keeping the Host CPU system from being overloaded. As more and more terminals are added, many systems cannot handle information in a timely manner. Response times have become a real problem. *quickly enough*

To make things worse, inaccurate data is sent over the communications lines with very little attempt to make it reasonable prior to sending. *as error-free as possible*

The DTI FORMS TERMINAL's design is an attempt to alleviate some of the tasks normally performed by the Host. *reduce + simplify*

KEYBOARD

The ninety-five-key keyboard provides a versatile tool for operator control of the various tasks that can be performed. The terminal can be used as "DUMB" terminal or a very smart terminal depending on the application.

EDITING

Extensive editing capability is provided so that typing or contents errors can be corrected prior to sending that information. *data to the Host.*

OPERATOR AIDS

has been made
Concern for making The terminal as friendly as possible has provided a Conversion Mode which makes it possible for the operator to convert representation in BINARY, DECIMAL, OCTAL, HEXADECIMAL or the ASCII symbol in any direction. *and display any character*

caps Ram memory contents can be read and altered at the keyboard. A non-destructive line ruler is provided as an aid to formatting the screen. A "Copy Line" function is provided to reduce typing when applicable. *time*

The previous field can be observed without destroying data or reserving a specified area of the screen for that purpose. *space*
MINISCREEN MODE

Any margins within the full screen area can be defined as the active screen area. The terminal functions are performed relative to this area when in the Mini-screen mode. While in the mode, the terminal acts as if this area were all it has to work with.

EXAMPLE 3

<u>72nd scale models</u>

TYPE	Price £
Fokker triplane	.95
Sopwith Camel	.95
DH88 Comet	.95
Douglas Skyraider	1.20
F4 Phantom	1.85
Short Stirling	4.10
Avro Lancaster	5.80
C130 Hercules	6.65
B17G Flying Fortress	2.40
F15a Eagle	3.20

EXAMPLE 4

EXERCISE 1

Integrate the following functions with respect to x:-

1) $x^3 + 3x^2 + x$

2) $2x^{3/2} - x^{-5/2} + 4$

3) $\dfrac{x^2 + 4x + 2}{x}$

4) $(x + 1)(x + 2)$

5) $(x^2 - 1)^2$

6) $\cos 4x - 3\sin 2x$

7) $\dfrac{\sec^2 2x}{2}$

8) $\dfrac{2 \tan 2x}{3}$

9) $3 \sec 6x$

144

EXAMPLE 5

EXAMPLE 6

THE WESTFIELD PLAYERS

Present

BONAVENTURE

A play

by Charlotte Hastings

Cast in order of appearance

Nurse Phillips	Joan Lawrence
Nurse Brent	Margaret Noakes
Sister Josephine	Shirley Wood
Willy Partridge	Howell Bolton-Jones
Sister Mary Bonaventure	Mary Howes
Dr.Jeffreys	Toby Moreton
The Mother Superior	Edna Greenland
Melling	Harry Saunders
Sarat Carn	Rachel Oliver
Miss Pierce	Joan Fisher
Martha Pentridge	Cynthia Brummitt

The Play produced by

FRANK JONES

Synopsis of scenes

The action of the play passes in the Convent of Our Lady of Rheims, a French Nursing Order, at Denzil St. David, a village some miles from Norwich, Emgland. The time is the present.

ACT I

The Hall of the Convent. About 6.00 p.m.

(Interval of six minutes)

ACT II

Scene 1 - Sister Mary's room. Two hours later.
Scene 2 - The same. Next evening.

(Interval of eight minutes)

ACT III

Scene 1 - The same. Next afternoon.
Scene 2 - The Hall of the Convent. Three hours later.

EXAMPLE 7

SALES FIGURES FOR 1983 - £000

DETAILS	MAIN PLANT	ASSOCIATED COMPANIES
Home Sales	10,560	9,789
Europe	8,876	5,897
Mid-East	2,345	1,231
Far East	987	3,123
U.S.A.	12,212	9,008
Russia	34	121

EXAMPLE 8

DATE	CHEQUE NO.	PAYEE	TOTAL	PURPOSE	AMOUNT	V.A.T.
1/10/83	12345	Emgas	67.89	Gas Bill	67.89	0.00
2/10/83	12346	R & S	13.80	Paper	12.00	1.80
2/10/83	12347	Cash	25.00	Self	25.00	0.00
3/10/83	12348	Rumbelows	14.49	TV Rent	12.60	1.89
10/10/83	12349	Marks & S	24.56	Food	24.56	0.00
11/10/83	12350	Jones	5.75	Petrol	5.00	0.75
13/10/83	12351	Smiths	161.00	Repairs	140.00	21.00
		TOTALS =	321.49		287.05	24.44

EXAMPLE 9

WEATHERFIELD TECHNICAL COLLEGE

Mid-Session Examination February 1984

Full-Time Basic Engineering Course

ENGINEERING SCIENCE

TIME ALLOWED:1 HOUR   ANSWER ALL QUESTIONS

ALL QUESTIONS CARRY EQUAL MARKS

ALL WORKING MUST BE SHOWN

1.   A car travels at a uniform speed of 40 Km/h. Calculate the distance travelled in one second and the time taken to travel 5 Km.

2.   A car has road wheels 65 cm in diameter, calculate the angular velocity of the wheels in radians per second at 40 Km/h.

3.   A mass of 400 Kg is lifted vertically by means of a chain. If the mass has a constant acceleration of 10 m/s/s, calculate the tension in the chain.

4.   Define "specific heat". Calculate the heat required to raise the temperature of 20 Kg of aluminium by 500 degrees Centigrade. The specific heat of aluminium may be taken as 0.21.

5.   Explain the difference between conductors and insulators. Give one example of a material which is a good conductor and one which is a good insulator.

6.   Explain the difference between "primary" and "secondary" cells and name one cell of each type.

7.   Define the terms "work" and "power". State one unit of each.

8.   Sketch the waveform of a sinusoidal current. If its periodic time is 10 milliseconds, calculate the frequency.

9.   Show by means of a diagram the shape and direction of a magnetic field due to a solenoid.

10.   A voltmeter of resistance 1000 ohms is connected in series with a resistor of 2000 ohms across the terminals of a d.c. supply. If the voltmeter reads 8 V what is the voltage of the supply ?

EXAMPLE 10

```
                                        The Stores
                                        23 Water Street
                                        LITTLEHALL
                                        Suffolk OK6 7DB

Ref PKW/TY

23 March 1984


K.L.Thompson & Son Ltd
23 York Street
HARBORN
South Yorkshire   Y09 4RF

For the attention of the Mail Order Department

Dear Sirs

Please send me as soon as possible to the above address   the
goods listed below:


14 pairs of Nylon Pillow Cases,  Style JJ54, @ £2.25 each
23 pairs of Nylon Single Sheets, Style JK55, @£14.45 each
 4 Duvet Covers, Cotton, double, Style YH44, @£23.60 each

We enclose a cheque for £458.25 in payment.

Yours faithfully
The Stores



P.K.Walters
Manager

enc
```

WORD-PROCESSING PACKAGES AVAILABLE IN THE UNITED KINGDOM

Name	Supplier	Notes
Address Book	Decision Technology	Mailing list manager
Applewriter	Pete & Pam	
Bookworm	Derwent Data	
BOS AutoWriter	MicroProducts	
Easy Speller	Soft Option	Add-on to Easywriter II
Easywriter	IBM	
Easywriter II	Soft Option	
Master Text	Asolv	
Magic Wand	Peachtree	
MicroSpell 86	Lifeboat	Spelling checker
Mailing List	TABS	Mailing list manager
MailMerge	MicroPro	Add-on to Wordstar
MemoPlan	Vector	
MultiMate	Ferrari	
Multi-Tool Word	Microsoft	Uses a 'mouse'
Palantir	Developed Software	
Perfect Writer	Perfect Software	
Perfect Speller	Perfect Software	Spelling checker for Perfect Writer
Postmaster	Lifeboat	
Power Text	Dexiver	
POPS	Peachtree	Spelling checker and mail list manager available
Screp	Stable Software	Designed for BBC Micro, tape and disk versions available
Select	Bonsai	

SM-Unitext	SM Software	Designed for use with Epson HX-20
Spectext	McGraw-Hill	Word processor for Sinclair Spectrum
Spellbinder	Encotel	
Spellstar	MicroPro	Spelling checker for Wordstar
SSI Wordperfect	DCC International	
Superscript	Precision Software	
Superspell	Precision Software	Spelling checker for Superscript
Superwriter	Pete & Pam	
Systematics Word Processor	Systematics	
T/Maker III	Lifeboat	Spreadsheet, list processor and file handler as well
TABWriter	TABS	
The Final Word	Promicro	
Textletter	Eduquest	Simple package for BBC Micros (A or B). Supplied on cassette
Textplus	Interactive Data	Includes merge, plot and filing features
Trendtext	Microtrend UK	Includes mail list manager
Vicwriter	Commodore	Designed for use with Vic-20
View	AcornSoft	Designed for use with BBC Micro
Visiword	Rapid Terminals	By designers of VisiCalc
Vizawrite 64	Viza Software	Designed for use with Commodore 64
Volkswriter	CACI	
Wordcraft 80	Dataview	
Word Plus PC	Wago Computers	Can be used with hard disk
Word Processor	Pete & Pan	
WordMaster	Soft Option	
Wordpro	Gemini Marketing	Cassette-based package for BBC Micro
Wordstar	Lifeboat	
Wordwise	Computer Concepts	ROM based for BBC Micro
WriteOn	Pete & Pam	

INDEX

Key names are shown in CAPITALS and refer only to the explanation of their use.
Page numbers in **bold** refer to words emboldened in text.